# Choosing Change

# Choosing Change

## How to Motivate Congregations to Face the Future

PETER D. COUTTS

ALBAN

Herndon, Virginia
www.alban.org

The Alban Institute
131 Elden St., Suite 202
Herndon, VA 20170

Unless otherwise noted, all Scripture quotations are from the New Revised Standard Version of the Bible, copyright © 1989, Division of Christian Education of the National Council of the Churches of Christ in the United States of America, and are used by permission.

Cover design by Daniel Belen, DBL Design Group.
Cover photo courtesty of Alvin Trusty. www.alvintrusty.com

Library of Congress Cataloging-in-Publication Data
    Coutts, Peter D.
    Choosing change : how to motivate congregations to face the future / Peter D. Coutts.
        pages cm
    Includes bibliographical references and index.
    ISBN 978-1-56699-437-8 (alk. paper)
    1. Christian leadership. 2. Change--Religious aspects--Christianity. 3. Change (Psychology)--Religious aspects--Christianity. I. Title.
    BV4509.5.C6775 2013
    253--dc23
                        2013015193

13  14  15  16  17      UBP      5  4  3  2  1

# Contents

# Foreword

As children of the Reformed faith family that traces its roots to early Reformation days in Geneva, Presbyterians are renowned for their emphasis on God's gracious sovereignty in the drama of human salvation. They have long cherished a slogan dating back to their earliest days: *Ecclesia reformata semper reformanda est secundum verbum Dei*, "The reformed church is always being reformed by the Word of God." In this formulation, God is the primary actor in the church's reform. So it might seem something of a surprise that a thoroughly Presbyterian church leader would pen a book focusing on how our choices matter critically in church reform.

But this is no ordinary Presbyterian. Reared among the minority of Canadian Presbyterians who chose in the 1920s to remain singularly "Reformed" rather than joining with the Methodists to form the United Church of Canada, Peter Coutts has emerged as a key twenty-first-century leader in the Presbyterian Church in Canada. He is first and foremost a pastor, who for years led one of its largest congregations—within walking distance from my wife's family home, so she and I have visited there frequently, witnessing firsthand some of the changes that he describes in the pages that follow.

Peter's winsome and effective deployment of pastoral energy, intelligence, imagination, and love has paved the way by which many other church leaders and congregations have sought him out as a trusted advisor, both within and beyond his denomination. What began for him as a serious effort to understand and implement congregational change locally has become a platform for widespread engagement with churches seeking transformation.

Years ago, Peter asked me why people who study church change don't pay more attention to motivation theory. He proposed that one reason many proponents of church change are less than fully effective in its actual implementation is a general failure to understand and address church members' motivations to change. It's rather like people knowing they need to lose weight and resolving to do so, yet failing to do so because of insufficient motivation to change their daily diet and exercise choices.

As a Reformed theologian, Peter is clear that the church's welfare is rooted in divine grace rather than human efforts. But he convincingly contends that the trajectory of the church as an organization is intimately connected to its members' choices. If a congregation wishes to transform its organizational life, its members must choose to do some new things. How do leaders motivate their congregants to make real and abiding changes in their shared life? This question led him to the world of motivation theory, and eventually to writing this book, which will prove to be an invaluable gift to congregations whose leaders digest and implement its insights.

Presbyterians love to quote the apostle Paul: "All things should be done decently and in order" (1 Corinthians 14:40). This book is a remarkable demonstration of Presbyterian commitment to carefully ordered thinking—Peter unpacks each step of the motivational change process clearly and thoroughly, aptly illustrating each with examples drawn from his extensive church experience.

This book unfolds an extended, richly nuanced congregational change process richly informed by motivational change theory and concrete church experience. While no single step of his process is itself difficult to grasp, the total journey requires close, extended attention. The effort to stick with it all the way through will repay the investment handsomely.

The numerous stories Peter tells from his own pastoral experience include failures as well as successes in implementing church change. This narrative honesty helps the reader identify with him more readily than if he had told only success stories.

It is tempting to cut to the chase in implementing change more quickly than Peter's plan entails. However, my own work in organizational change at both congregational and regional church levels confirms that taking the time and trouble to lay out the preparatory groundwork he advocates bears great dividends in securing the desired outcome. Indeed, while Peter's work focuses particularly on congregations, regional judicatory leaders will find that his process is equally helpful for engaging change in their organizations, which are often even more change-resistant than congregations. Many failures that have befallen well-intentioned church change projects might have been averted had the change leaders been more attentive to prepare their institution well through the pre-contemplation, discovery, dialogue, and deliberation stages that precede actual change implementation in this model.

One area in which this book is especially helpful is in dealing productively with change resistance—a problem that anyone seeking to effect church change will certainly face. By providing clear pathways for positive engagement with those who are late or who steadfastly refuse to buy in to change, Peter helps congregational leaders map out and implement change that will prove more durable than would be the case were such folk simply dismissed from the process.

While this book's methodology could well be effective for shaping transformation in many types of organizations, its consistent tight focus specifically on congregational change renders it singularly helpful to church leaders. Peter is acutely attuned to the drivers and resisters that crop up particularly in congregational change efforts, rendering his roadmap for institutional change especially helpful to those seeking to transform the life and mission of worshiping communities.

This book lays out astute, accessible, step-by-step, practical guidance to church leaders seeking to expand their body's missional capacities. Wise pastoral leaders will want also to offer clear and compelling theological underpinnings for proposed church reforms. While such theological rationale lies beyond this book's immediate scope, Peter recognizes its pastoral necessity, and thus offers a robust theological and biblical grounding for his motivational change process in supplemental materials posted on the book's website, www.choosingchange. ca. It is critical not only that church leaders advance their desired changes with close attention to institutional change dynamics, but also that they interpret such changes in terms of the reformation God is continually working to accomplish in the church.

*Sheldon W. Sorge*
*General Minister and Executive of the Pittsburgh Presbytery*
*Presbyterian Church (U.S.A.)*

# Acknowledgments

Writing a book is like taking a very long journey, and receiving support along the way is necessary if the writer is to have any hope of reaching the destination. I wish to thank the many people who contributed in their own unique ways to this book. First among them are the congregations I have served: Saanich Peninsula Presbyterian Church (Sidney, BC), Oakridge Presbyterian Church (London, ON), and St. Andrew's Presbyterian Church (Calgary, AB). I am grateful for their encouragement and support as I learned the ways of ministry and the practice of leadership. I am especially grateful for the support of St. Andrew's as I wrote this book. Many people took an ongoing interest in this project and provided great encouragement. Thank you.

This journey actually began in the late 1990s when I was casting about for a topic for my DMin dissertation. I spent about a year at McCormick Seminary in Chicago pondering the question, How do I help someone begin a new pursuit in faith? In time the answer came to me: by encouraging and facilitating the choices people make. Professor Deborah Kapp, my thesis advisor, helped me find several highways and byways in my introduction to the psychology of motivation. With her assistance I explored how congregations can motivate individuals to make choices to do something new in faith. What began as a thesis topic became an ongoing academic interest that eventually evolved into an interest in how to help entire congregations choose to do something new. I am grateful to Professor Kapp for her part in my discovery of what has become my abiding interest.

All long journeys need times of respite. In 2008 I was privileged to receive one of seven Pastoral Study Project Grants from the Louisville Institute. These grants are made available annually to "academic practitioners" to "support the intellectual work of pastoral leaders who have the capacities for research, teaching, and writing that can reach broad audiences."[1] This grant provided me with the opportunity to take a research and writing sabbatical in 2009. I am grateful to the Louisville Institute for their support of this project. The grant was made possible through the generosity of the Lilly Endowment, which supports the institute's many programs.

A good journey is shared with wayfarers who join in the travels for a time. This book has relied on the work of many academics in the fields of psychology, sociology, organization development, leadership, and theology. I am particularly indebted to Professor Jackson Carroll of Duke Divinity School, who in kindness read a portion of this book and made comments on my use of his research. My thinking has also been shaped by many hours of conversation with colleagues in ministry who know the realities of congregational change from their day-to-day experience. In particular I am grateful to my friends in ministry who are always generous in sharing their wisdom: Stuart Macdonald, John-Peter Smit, Victor Kim, as well as Sabrina and Terry Ingram.

Writing a book is one thing, but having it published is a very different thing. The Alban Institute responded so quickly and positively to my book proposal that I found myself simultaneously excited and intimidated! Their agreement to publish this book meant that my journey actually had a destination. I am grateful for the confidence the Alban Institute has had in me and this project. I am also incredibly grateful for the gift Alban gave me in my editor, Beth Gaede. While I have written much over the years, Beth taught me how to write a book. She also became my first grammar teacher since grade school, which I apparently needed. This book is a much better book than it would have been because of her significant help.

Finally, I am most grateful to my family, who were my constant companions on this four-year journey. No words can express my thankfulness for the generosity and patience they showed me throughout the time I took to write. The love and support of my wife, Sheri, and our sons, Paul and Daniel, carried me when my enthusiasm for this project waned. This book would not exist without them.

*Soli Deo gloria!*

# PART 1

---

# AN INTRODUCTION TO MOTIVATION THEORY

## CHAPTER 1

# What Is Motivation and Why Is It Important?

*Leadership is influence—nothing more, nothing less.*[1]
*—John C. Maxwell*

Why are you reading this book? The simple answer is because you are motivated to read it.

Imagine this scenario. Perhaps you are concerned that your congregation is reticent to address needed change. Perhaps you are concerned your approach to leadership misses the mark somehow, and you think you need to enhance your understanding of leadership in order to benefit your congregation. Needs are motives that we can experience as a feeling of concern, and concern pushes us to take action. Perhaps you hope that the congregation's need can be addressed by helping the congregation fulfill more fully one of Christ's callings to the church. These callings are values, and values are motives that can draw us forward into action. Motives that pull us toward change are experienced as a feeling of hope.

But perhaps your past experience has dampened your hope that the congregation can make needed change, and so you feel a bit frustrated and despondent—unmotivated. Then, perhaps, the title of this book caught your eye and you thought to yourself, "Motivation is what our congregation needs!" You began to think that the content of this book might help you to help the congregation appreciate more deeply the current concerns and to discover greater hope. So you begin to trust this book to improve your leadership and that trust strengthens your own hope that the congregation will change. So now you are reading this book.

How closely did this hypothetical scenario reflect the reasons for your own choice to read this book? My hunch is that it does to some degree, because this scenario outlines how motivation operates within all of us.

Motives are the reasons behind what we do. Motives influence us to approach outcomes we want or avoid outcomes we don't want. They stir us up to the point of feeling compelled or excited to do something. We are aroused to take action when we have sufficient motives with sufficient influence to prompt us to move in a certain direction, which is typically toward attaining some goal. When we are moved into action by our motives, our behavior is said to be *motivated*. Put the other way around, we motivate people by appealing to their motives.

Albert Bandura—perhaps the world's greatest living psychologist— defines motivation this way: "Motivation is a general construct that encompasses a system of self-regulatory mechanisms."[2] In other words, *motivation* is a general term used like a corral to hold in one common place the many psychological processes that influence our attitudes, intentions, choices, and actions. Now while this is an accurate defini- tion of motivation, it is not such a useful one for the purpose of this book. Rather, we will use a more popular definition. Here we will think of motivation as *the degree of arousal to act*. Any of us—in any situation, at any particular time, for any specific issue—will be more or less influenced to take certain actions by the degree of motivation we have to do so. The English word *motivation* is derived from the Latin word *movere*, which means "to move." When we have more motivation we are more likely to act.

In my youth I had a toy rocket that could fly. To make it work, I had to squeeze the plastic rocket tightly onto its valve launcher, which was connected to a hand pump. Pumping forced air into the rocket. The friction between the rocket and the valve launcher was quite high, however, so I had to pump and pump to increase the air pressure to the point where the force of the air pressure promoting flight exceeded the frictional force that resisted flight. When that tipping point was attained, the force of the compressed air released the rocket to create a dramatic launch and rapid movement. Let's think of motivation in a similar way: it is the degree of pressure we feel to act or the degree of friction we feel that prompts us not to act. Motivation can be understood as a psychological state, relative to a particular action, that prompts us to either approach or avoid that action.

I began this chapter with the question, Why are you reading this book? Answering the question why gets at our motives. Motives are influences that can cause our motivation to increase or decrease. Thinking back to the hypothetical scenario used in the beginning of this chapter, the motives causing your feelings of concern and the motives causing your feelings of hope may have promoted your choice to read right now. But other motives may also have been at work, ones that act like the friction in my toy rocket, perhaps enticing you to simply relax and watch your favorite TV show instead. Our motives often influence us by simultaneously promoting and resisting a specific action. But for you in this moment right now, the balance of your motives and the strength of those motives have led to the choice to read. The role of motives will be explored fully in chapter 2.

*Our motivation*, however, does not rise and fall exclusively on the ever-shifting influence of *our motives*. Several self-regulatory psychological mechanisms can moderate the motivation that comes from our motives, and these can also cause motivation to increase or decrease. The opening scenario illustrated one such moderator. Experience can dampen people's confidence in their ability to help lead change. Our confidence to act is rooted in our *capability beliefs*, which are the beliefs that we actually can do what we want to do. Low capability beliefs moderate motivation by reducing it, even if motives for action are substantial and influential. Conversely, high capability beliefs create confidence that we can do what we are motivated to do.

Another moderator of motivation is *context beliefs*. The context for congregational change could be the neighborhood, the wider community, the denomination, or the culture of the wider society. The issue here is whether one believes the context will allow something to happen or prevent it from happening. Belief that the context will not be a negative influence moderates motivation by increasing it. Belief that the context will have a negative impact moderates motivation by decreasing it. Moderators of motivation, such as capability and context beliefs, will be explored more fully in chapter 3.

So, if you haven't done so already, please pause for a moment and ask yourself the question, Why am I reading this book? If you dig deep in answering it, you will probably discover that more was behind your decision to read this book than you first imagined. But that is, in part, how motivation works in us. Motivation typically influences us behind the scenes in our subconscious, even though it can lead to a conscious act like physically picking up this book five minutes ago. Without motivation, this book would still be on the shelf, and you could be watching a sitcom.

The purpose of this book is to help you learn about the psychology of motivation, and the goal of that learning is for you to become a better leader. If motivation is the degree of arousal to act and leadership is about moving people to act in new ways, then leaders are in the motivation business.

So let's think about another question: To what degree do I as a congregational leader consider the motives and motivation among the people of my congregation as I try to encourage change in their behavior? Many leaders do not think about motivation. For them, encouraging change is about selling their congregation on a new idea, governed by the assumption that a better idea should win the day. But wide experience in communities of faith indicates that this approach often doesn't work and leaves many congregational leaders frustrated and demoralized. They see the need for change in their congregation, and they earnestly want to help their congregation change. But many leaders find that the approach to leadership they learned, which perhaps worked better in days gone by, is just not working so well for them now. So let's think about that question again: To what degree do I consider the motives and motivations in my congregation as I try to encourage change in its behavior? The premise of this book is that with greater understanding of a motivational approach to leadership and by applying this approach, we can improve our ability to lead.

## An Invitation to Think
## Differently about Leadership

Many congregational leaders are stumped about how congregational change occurs. The first church I served had started life six years earlier as a satellite congregation of the big church downtown. What began as a group of thirty people in 1982 had declined to eleven by the time I arrived in 1987 to serve as the first minister for this newly independent church plant. Despite the decline, the congregation was pretty content with its course. I was appointed to the congregation for the express purpose of changing that course: to help them grow, develop greater vitality, and build their own facility to set them on a path for a stronger future. One of the first things I knew this congregation needed to do was move. The congregation met in the chapel of a funeral home because it was rent free. But since Christianity is about a resurrection, the current home seemed to me to send the wrong message.

This wasn't the only wrong message the congregation was sending. When I arrived on my first Sunday, I found that the pulpit in the chapel was wrapped in a tartan cloth. Canadian Presbyterians may have a strong Scottish heritage, but this was the most startling expression of those roots I'd ever seen in a congregation! Over the following weeks I learned the story about the tartan drape. Years before, the congregation had met at another place where the upright piano sat with its back exposed to the worshipers. Most worshipers deemed this unsightly, and they agreed that a drape should be made to cover the whole back of the piano. The person who volunteered to make the drape had strong nostalgic ties to her Scottish background, so she chose a tartan cloth for the project. When the congregation moved from that location to the funeral home chapel, the drape was no longer needed because the piano in the chapel was not exposed. But now the congregation had this drape and a tradition of displaying it at worship. So the question naturally arose: How could they use the drape now? The answer: Use it to decorate the pulpit. The fact that a pulpit is much smaller than a piano did not deter them. If it enclothed the pulpit to the point that the pulpit could no longer be seen, that was OK. The tradition was maintained, and the drape got a promotion. This object and practice was meaningful for my new congregation.

As soon as I saw the tartan drape, I knew it had to go. To me it was sending the wrong message to first-time worshipers—"This congregation is for Scots only"—and that message wouldn't help the congregation grow. So, when I had sufficient courage, I ventured into my first change initiative in the life of my first congregation. I proposed that we no longer put the drape out when we set up the chapel for our services. The idea was gently, politely, and unanimously dismissed. I pointed out to the congregation that because the original reason for using the drape was no longer an issue, we no longer needed it. They smiled and still said no. I explained my thinking that it might be a turnoff to first-time visitors, but in answer they said, "But the people who are here now like it!" Our eleven folk were so kind to me in this discussion, but if the occasion had a theme song it was, "We Shall Not Be Moved." A few months later we relocated to a Seventh-day Adventist Church. On the first Sunday in our new home, the drape could not be found, to the disappointment of all, and it was never replaced—at my encouragement. What happened to it? I took it during the move. For many years, it served as the skirt around the base of our family Christmas trees.

I am not proud of this story. This failure gave me my first practical lesson in congregational leadership: the right idea presented rationally does not always influence people to adopt new directions, even when the proposal seems to make so much sense to the leader. Since I failed to persuade, I made an autocratic decision on the congregation's behalf. In fact, I acted against the choice of the congregation. But I also tried to use another external force. As a leader, I was trying to persuade the congregation to adopt my motives, which were completely external to them. Instead, I should have been thinking about the congregation's internal forces, the congregants' own motives and how I could influence motives already present so they might give those motives different priorities, which might in turn lead the congregation to make its own choice to give me the tartan drape to use as my Christmas tree skirt. "Leadership is influence—nothing more, nothing less." Leaders encourage and facilitate congregational change by influencing the internal motivation within the people of the congregation so that they choose to change themselves. This is motivational leadership.

## The Impact of Our
## Culture of Choice on Congregations

Years ago a ministry student was leading Sunday worship in three small, rural congregations. A part-time student was all the congregations could afford. They were content with the arrangement, until the student's graduation day loomed near. "We don't want you to go!" they pleaded. He responded, "My family can't live on what you can afford to pay me." "Listen," they said, "we will do anything to keep you here." The student minister paused and then asked, "Anything?" It was the turning point in the history of these congregations. The three congregations united, sold their historic buildings, and began worshiping in a school gym. They quickly changed their worship style from their age-old traditional format to a contemporary one complete with digital projectors and praise music. Clergy robes were replaced by golf shirts and chinos. Sermons focused on real life and practical Christian answers for living. Not all the original members liked the big changes, and some moved on. But the majority appreciated the changes, which also drew newcomers to join them. In six years the congregation's worship attendance grew from sixty-one to more than seven hundred people per week.

At the same time, a pastor a four-hour drive away was trying to do the same thing with the three small, rural congregations he served. This pastor had a similar vision for dramatic renewal centered on amalgamation (merger) and instituting a contemporary worship style that would appeal to younger people. These congregations were reluctant but still agreed to a trial merger. As for the contemporary service, however, the members thought it would be OK to offer one, but not as a replacement to their traditional Sunday worship. So the pastor started a weeknight service in the same format as in the first story. Soon it too became successful beyond all expectations. At one point this service was drawing one-quarter of all the teenagers who lived in the region. The impact was significant enough that the region's coordinator of youth hockey called the pastor to confirm what night the service would be held during the next season. It seemed that worship was cutting into attendance at practices.

Now, can you imagine in Canada hockey practices being rescheduled to accommodate a worship service? For many Canadians this is its own kind of heresy. Even so, the congregation was indifferent, at best, about the midweek service, despite its apparent success. Many thought the loud volume of the music was undignified. They did not appreciate the physical changes that were made to their traditional sanctuary to accommodate the band and technology. Some members resented the fact that their offerings were paying for this service, which was also taking "their" minister away from them. Many worried that there might be a move to bring contemporary worship to Sunday morning. Additionally, the trial merger was not going so well. Some infighting broke out among those vying for control of the amalgamated congregation, with the losers stoking fires of discontent. In the end the pastor left. Two congregations merged, mainly because one could not afford the necessary renovations to its historic building. The third congregation was simply content to die.

Two similar situations were served by similar forward-looking, visionary, and energetic pastoral leaders who wanted to implement the same kind of change. So why would the outcomes be so dramatically different? It came down to the very different choices these congregations made regarding their futures.

Now humans have been choice makers since the days when hunter-gatherers had to decide when to hunt and what to gather. Choice making has been a part of the Christian faith ever since Jesus extended an invitation to four fishermen to "follow me." Making choices is what humans do. But over time, people in Western society have gained ever-increasing autonomy, personal authority, and opportunity to be choice makers. The development of democracy since the seventeenth century and the rise of consumerism since industrialization in the nineteenth century have strengthened our belief in ourselves as choice makers. Since World War II a third influence has been added: the growth of individualism as the cultural norm. Today individuals feel more personal autonomy and power to choose than ever before in human history.

The impact of our choice-making culture on congregational life in North America and Western Europe over the past sixty years has been significant, prompting a lot of sociological research in the attempt to understand and explain it. Sociologist Peter Berger, for example, wrote as early as 1963 that people choose which church to attend by conducting their own market analysis of the available congregations to determine which church suits them best.[3] Today we call it church shopping, and most of us have probably done it at least once in our lives.

Since then, sociologists have observed the strengthening trend toward individualism and choice making and their growing impact on congregational life. In 1987 Wade Clark Roof and William McKinney described the cultural changes this way:

> Americans generally hold a respectful attitude toward religion, but also they increasingly regard it as a matter of personal choice or preference. Today choice means more than simply having an op-tion among religious alternatives; it involves religion as an option itself and opportunity to draw selectively off a variety of traditions in the pursuit of self.[4]

A decade later Wade Clark Roof wrote of this deepening trend, calling the cultural context for churches a "spiritual marketplace."[5] He wrote, "Earlier in an industrial society, personal identities were linked to production; one's occupation or profession was a major source of a relatively stable identity. But beginning with the post–World War II United States, personal identities came to be linked more to lifestyle and consumption."[6] In other words, personal identity today is shaped more and more by what I want for myself.

The highly respected psychologist Martin Seligman sums up the cultural changes of recent decades very pointedly. He has written that the shifts in our behavior are the consequence of a fundamental change in our own psychology.

For the first time in history—because of technology and mass production and distribution—large numbers of people are able to have
a significant measure of choice and therefore personal control over
their lives. Not the least of these choices concerns our own habits
of thinking. By and large, people have welcomed this control. We
belong to a society that grants to its individual members powers they
have never had before, a society that takes individuals' pleasures
and pains very seriously, that exalts the self and deems personal
fulfillment a legitimate goal, an almost sacred right.[7]

Given this shift, it is no wonder that the church experiences the
struggles it does today. One major consequence has been mainline
church decline. My own denomination—the Presbyterian Church in
Canada—marked in 1958 the historic highpoint for the number of
infants baptized in one year. But after that year, the annual number
of baptisms dropped dramatically, far faster than the decline in the
birthrate of the baby boom. Our historic highpoint for confirmation (a
time when teens make personal profession of their faith) also turned
out to be 1958. Over a period of fifteen years the number of baptisms
and confirmations per year declined by more than 50 percent. Church
school enrollment did the same. All of a sudden, starting in the late
1950s, adults were encouraging, permitting, or condoning a new
degree of permissiveness for their children, and new choices were
being made regarding the personal importance of faith and church
involvement. Today our denomination is less than half the size it was
fifty years ago. Other mainline denominations across North America
have experienced similar decline.

The development of a choice-making culture in our society has
also had an impact on those who have remained in congregations.
Take, for example, the prevalence of conflict in congregations today.
In a 2004 survey published by *Christianity Today*, 95 percent of the
responding pastors said they had experienced congregational conflict
of some kind. Twenty percent reported that they were currently engaged in a congregational conflict, which suggests how prevalent conflicts are within North American congregations. The most common
conflicts were over the common choices congregations have to make:
vision and direction (64 percent), who should be the congregation's

leaders (43 percent), and how to allocate the congregation's finances (33 percent). The most prevalent kind of conflict, however, was over who gets to make the choices: 85 percent of the respondents said they had experienced conflict over "control issues."[8] Congregational conflicts are typically fights over choices. Conflict does not affect just congregations—it also affects whole denominations. We need only note with sorrow how conflicts over homosexuality are tearing entire denominations apart today. Today denominational doctrine and policy seems more often to divide rather than unite.

Ultimately, cultural change necessitates a change in how congregational leaders lead. In an individualistic society, today's leaders need to work harder than in the past at building consensus. Theologian Johannes van der Ven has written about the impact our choice-making culture has had on the church. He believes there is a growing tendency of people to approach the church with an "attitude of calculation." He defines this as "the process through which the societal and personal interaction between people is determined to an increasing extent by the calculative weighing of costs and benefits."[9] Recall our definition of motives as the reasons behind what we do. Motives influence us to approach outcomes we want or to avoid outcomes we don't want. This is what Van der Ven is observing, but he is also suggesting that over time this "calculative weighing" seems to have shifted slowly, subtly, but steadily to weighing the costs and benefits in an ever more self-serving way. Consequently, Van der Ven sees within Christianity a rising priority on the individual that can make the individual more important than either the consensus view of the community of faith or the ideals of the Christian faith itself. Van der Ven observes the consequence of this trend: "It does not leave the church untouched. Not only do people meet the church proceeding from an attitude of calculation, but the church itself does not seem to be able to escape it."[10] The church in Western society has been caught up in the currents of cultural change and is drawn along and affected by these currents. The rise in the individual's freedom and power to make choices is consequently making the relationship between congregant and congregation more conditional, negotiated, and transactional in nature.[11]

We live in a fully democratized, consumer-oriented society in which people believe they have the autonomous power to make choices, including within the realm of religious belief, practice, and participation. Over the past generation this belief has been trending upward, and the trend does not appear to be abating. This is the cultural context faith communities in North America operate within now, and it has implications for congregational life. When it comes to congregational leadership in particular, the implications are twofold: leaders need to understand how people make choices and then understand how to influence those choices. In other words, leaders need a motivational view of leadership.

It seems that clergy today understand that motivation is a part of leadership. In 2006 sociologist Jackson Carroll published an excellent study of American clergy and their congregations that explored in part how leadership is understood by clergy today. The study showed that a majority of pastors prefer a motivating leadership style. Seventy percent of the respondents agreed with the statement, "I try to inspire and encourage lay members to make decisions and take action, although I will take action alone if I believe it is needed."[12] To *inspire* is to arouse people, to influence or guide them. To *encourage* is to promote, to advance, and to urge. All these activities seek to build motivation in people to choose a new direction and commit to attain it. Apparently almost three-quarters of pastors want to express a motivating style of leadership.

But Carroll's study also tells us that this is not easy.[13] Thirty percent of the surveyed clergy said that their congregation's sense of direction was either very vague or altogether absent. Forty-nine percent of the surveyed clergy agreed that "we have a clear vision but not enough commitment to achieve it."[14] As we saw above, motivation stands behind our intentions to do something new and energizes us to act on what we intend. So according to the survey, 79 percent of congregations do not have sufficient motivation either to create or clarify a sense of direction or to act on the direction they have.

Clergy today recognize the impact our individualistic culture of choice has on congregations. They appreciate a need for a motivational style of leadership. They also understand how hard it is to motivate congregations. Given all this, I am more than a little surprised that the psychology of motivation has not gained greater presence in leadership books.

This book seeks to fill the gap. What follows is an overview of some current thinking from the field of motivation psychology. We will isolate some important theories, ideas, and terms that are most pertinent for leaders who desire to encourage congregational change. These will be examined in the first half of the book so that you will have the concepts you will need for the second half of the book, which focuses on application.

An additional book chapter, a theology of motivation, is online at the website for *Choosing Change*: www.choosingchange.ca. The site contains extra articles and resources, as well as a reproducible version of the "Readiness for Change Questionnaire," found later in this book. The Bible is a wonderful primer on the topics of motives, attitudes, and intentions—both ours and God's. From its pages we can derive a theology of motivation that is rooted in three central concepts of our faith: stewardship, hope, and trust. I hope you turn to that resource as well, since this book refers to these concepts regularly.

## CHAPTER 2

---

# Stewardship and Hope at Work: The Origins of Motivation

*There is nothing as practical as a good theory.*[1]
—*Kurt Lewin*

How motives come to influence us is not a simple, straightforward thing. To help you out, here is an outline of the motivation theory that we will work through in this chapter:

- Motives are simply reasons to act, but on their own they really don't have any motivating power.
- A motive become motivating when it is evaluated through the formation of an attitude, which can determine that a motive needs to be acted on.
- Attitudes—which can be empowered motives—influence the development of intention, which is a readiness to act.
- When intention is combined with the belief that one is able to do what one intends, it leads to goal commitment and the choice to act on one's motives.

## The Psychology of Motives

Motives either push us into action or pull us into action. So let's start by looking more closely at how motives work and how leaders can influence them.

My city of Calgary recently introduced curbside recycling. Alberta's other large city, Edmonton, initiated it more than twenty years ago, so why so slow here? The motives of Calgarians. One reason for the delay was probably that many people did not see a need to develop curbside recycling. For many years Calgary has had a large number of neighborhood recycling depots. Residents need only load up their recyclables in their vehicle, haul them off to a depot, and then sort the various materials into the appropriate bins. In the minds of many people the need (which is a motive) was being met, and the value for environmental care (which is a motive) was being expressed in the present practices. Motives motivate people into action, but unless our motives change, our choices remain the same and our actions remain the same. Why fix what's not broken?

But the system was broken; at least that's what the city's waste management people thought. They saw an enormous amount of recyclable material going into the dump daily. This was not good environmental stewardship. It also added to the cost of waste management and shortened the lifespan of the landfill site. The managers of waste management had several motives that gave them concern and that motivated them to find a solution to what they perceived to be problems.

They captured their solution in a goal: to reduce by 80 percent the amount of material going into the landfill site by 2020. Goals provide the focus for our hopes, because goals represent how we plan to satisfy our motives. But what path should be taken to fulfill that goal? Well, there are actually quite a lot of serious as well as harebrained ways to accomplish this goal. The city could fire garbage into outer space, but that would be pretty expensive. Garbage could be shipped to the United States, but that would anger Calgary's neighbors to the south. We could dump it in our Bow River, ending the landfill problem but creating a water pollution problem. You get the idea. Not only is our choice of goal shaped by our motives but so is the path we choose to attain a goal, and the motives affecting goal choice may be quite different from the motives affecting the path choice. Waste management decided to introduce curbside recycling as the path because of the motives of practicality and cost effectiveness.

To see this goal adopted and this plan implemented, waste management had to influence city council so that the council would approve it. City councilors, like everyone else, harbor a collection of motives. In any given situation, only a few motives from that bank of motives will apply. Among those few motives, some will have a greater priority than others. In fact, different motives can be in opposition to each other, leaving us feeling conflicted. So it was with Calgary's city council. For them, environmental stewardship was a good and important motive. Extending the life of the landfill site was also a good motive because of the cost and headache of finding and developing a new site. These motives moved the council toward waste management's plan. But they also harbored motives that pushed them in the opposite direction. This new program would cost a bunch of money, and the council was committed to fiscal restraint. The value for fiscal restraint was a motive. Then there was the not-so-insignificant issue of reelection. If councilors approved this project and angered the citizens, then that might result in not being reelected. Motives of self-interest are real, many, and powerful. These city councilors had to weigh the merit and importance of several competing motives, which is something we all experience at times. In some situations a motive, or more commonly a collection of motives, will surface naturally to gain priority over other motives, which in turn will influence our decisions, intentions, and actions. But in other situations, sorting through our motives is not so easy, and we are forced to struggle with them in order to make a decision. On those occasions we choose to give priority and power to some motives over others. The city council chose to adopt and give priority to the motives of waste management and approved the program. This is one way change begins to happen: when people choose to adopt the motives of others.

The first hurdle was crossed, but if the program was going to work, the people of Calgary would have to buy into it and participate. This presented a different motivational problem, because the motives that motivated waste management and city council probably wouldn't motivate the citizens. For instance, citizens could assume that the motive of environmental stewardship was being satisfied quite well through the current system of depots. In addition, the budget problems of waste management and timelines for the landfill site would probably be meaningless to ordinary citizens. In other words, waste management appreciated that they probably could not easily influence people to adopt the motives of waste management. So what waste management had to do was find and highlight the motives already harbored in Calgarians in order to influence people's participation in curbside recycling. We call this *appealing* to people's motives.

Waste management started a promotional program to appeal to specific motives. The biggest one was the convenience of the new program. Transporting recyclables to a depot was a nuisance, especially when the temperature is -30°C (-22°F) in the middle of our long winter. Having recyclables picked up curbside was certainly appealing. It would also be convenient because sorting recyclables would no longer be required—something that had to be done at the depots. It was also promoted as a free program: the sixty-gallon bin would be delivered free to homes, and recyclables would be picked up weekly at no charge. Everybody finds "free" an appealing idea. The motives of convenient-for-me and no-cost-to-me reside in our collection of motives all the time. Overall, the most prominent motives highlighted in the promotional campaign appealed to the self-interest of people.

But waste management also highlighted important values that act as motives. They highlighted the value for environmental stewardship and educated Calgarians about the ineffectiveness of the current recycling system. They spoke of the environmental impact of creating a new landfill site, something the environmentally conscious would want to avoid. The promotions also highlighted the significant cost of opening a new landfill site, to appeal to those motivated to keep their property taxes low. If waste management wanted to motivate Calgarians, then waste management needed to appeal to the motives of citizens.

Six months into the new program waste management was able to report that the amount of material being recycled had doubled. It was a success, but not quite: the new higher participation rate would still not meet the target goal of reducing by 80 percent the amount of material going into the landfill site by 2020. After all, the program is voluntary. Calgary's waste management is now considering two follow-up interventions. One is an additional program that will collect organic household waste separately at curbside to be composted. The other possible intervention is to charge households for their nonrecyclable garbage. If you had to pay for the garbage you put out, how diligent would you become in recycling? Some motives are more motivating than others.

Let's summarize what we've learned here about motives. The story of Calgary recycling illustrates several different kinds of motives, both to maintain the status quo and to change. Motives can be

- needs ("How am I going to get rid of all this stuff?")
- values ("Human waste is killing the environment, so doing our best to recycle is vital.")
- incentives ("People will recycle more if there is a curbside program that doesn't require sorting.")
- personal goals ("If I promote curbside recycling, that will help me get reelected to city council next year.")
- preferences ("Given the choice, I'd prefer the city to take my recyclables away than my having to haul them away.")
- costs ("Do I really want to pay an extra eight dollars per month in taxes for this service?")
- the avoidance of negative outcomes ("I don't want to pay two bucks a bag for my garbage, so I'd better recycle.")

Further, in any given situation some motives (for example, "Keep the tax rate low") will have greater priority than others (for example, "I want a more convenient solution to recycling"). Each of us harbors a large number of complementary and competing interconnected motives. Imagine your bundle of motives to be like a bale of hay. At any particular time you may be conscious of only a few of your motives, and among them some will have a greater priority than others. Using our analogy, at any particular time only a few straws will be poking up out of the bale, and some will poke up higher and more noticeably than the others. The motives you are aware of, as well as their priority, can be challenged and changed moment by moment. This happens because a new thought or a new situation presents itself.

So far we have only considered how individuals deal with their motives. Now imagine what happens in a group of individuals. Each person harbors a large number of complementary and competing interwoven motives. If an individual's motives are like a bale of hay, then a congregation is like a barn full of bales. Individuals are motivated when sufficient motives come to have sufficient influence that they move people into action. Congregations—as a collection of individuals—are moved into action when sufficient *common* motives come to have sufficient influence.

Given what we have seen up to this point, encouraging a group of people to change can suddenly appear pretty impossible because those many bales of hay include a whole lot of unique stalks. Fortunately, there is something that helps us: culture. The fact that a congregation has a culture means that to some degree, congregants share beliefs, values, priorities, and norms of behavior. A shared culture also means that congregants share motives: needs, values, incentives, goals, aversion to certain negative outcomes, and so on. When encouraging change, the leaders' job is to find those few stalks of straw common to as many bales as possible and draw them out as far as possible in order for these motives to motivate the congregation to move in the same direction on the path to change.

Congregational change requires congregants to reflect on their motives. My hunch is that a minority of congregations ever consciously consider their motives. For example, many congregations are motivated tacitly by the goal of maintaining comfort for those who form the congregation today. But if a congregation wishes to express more fully its nature as the body of Christ and its sharing in the *missio Dei*, it needs to consider why it does what it does today and why it might want to do things differently tomorrow. Going back to our analogy, leadership is about helping congregants see which straws are sticking out of their bale today, evaluate whether these are the ones they want sticking out, and then make changes so the congregation will have stronger motivation to carry out faithful ministry tomorrow. Congregants can be encouraged to reflect on their motives through the age-old practices of faith nurture: reading Scripture, preaching, prayer, reflection, and discernment. Reflecting on motives through these spiritual practices, in turn, can help congregants reconsider their stewardship in the present (making them more aware of *push* motives) as well as their hopes for tomorrow (making them more aware of *pull* motives). Both are important for change to happen.

Psychology professor Gabriele Oettingen at New York University is interested in how people actually form concrete goals and commit to them. She has found that change happens most easily when people are aware and motivated by both push and pull motives. The "mental contrast," as she calls it, between an unpreferred present and a preferred future creates a dissonance that people find uncomfortable and in need of resolution. This need creates the motivation to change.[2]

But there is another reason why emphasizing both kinds of motives simultaneously is important. When considering change, some people have a natural inclination to strive after benefits and improvements. These people are said to have a promotion focus, because their attention is grabbed by what can be gained in change. They are more inclined toward hopefulness, more motivated by goals, and more likely to anticipate a positive outcome in change. In other words, they respond best to pull motivations. In contrast, a significant proportion of a congregation is more concerned with security. Rather than focusing on possible gains, their attention is grabbed by potential losses. They are motivated to avoid negative outcomes. These people have a prevention focus, which means they are moved more by concerns arising from current reality and respond better to push motivations. Goals, for them, are not seen as positive futures to strive toward as much as they are seen as solutions to the current problems that need to be avoided.[3] The promotion or prevention focus of people is another reason why leaders need to speak *to* concerns about both current reality and hopes for the future, because people tend to become more engaged by talk of one more than talk of the other.

## Push Motives and Current Reality

*Concern* is an evaluative feeling that something in current reality is no longer helpful, constructive, or right. Concern arises from push motives. We can experience it as anxiety, guilt, fear, or anger. It is a desire to see the object of our concern changed. It prompts a willingness to accept change and to participate in the work of change. A poor performance review at work can cause sufficient concern for an employee that she changes her work habits. The cardiologist's assessment can cause sufficient concern for a man that he changes his lifestyle to avoid a heart attack. Concerns are a part of life for all of us and regularly drift through our consciousness. When a concern becomes compelling enough, it fosters intentions to change.

It seems to me, however, that some writers on leadership want to bypass the motivational power of concern. Philosophically, they would like all the motivation to come from the appeal of goals. In addition, congregational leaders can be shy about eliciting concerns regarding current reality, because they think negative talk might become a self-fulfilling prophecy. It is also understandable that leaders would rather not create anxiety, guilt, fear, or anger. Perhaps some also worry that concern could get out of hand, with fear developing into panic and anger becoming outrage. Yet, people who have sincere concern appreciate that something in current reality needs to change, and they desire something be done about it. Concern can foster ownership—and stewardship—of the issues of current reality.

Stewardship is about accepting responsibility for something that has been entrusted to one's care and then taking the initiative to ensure its preservation and growth. Parents, for example, are stewards of their children. When we become a steward, we become attentive to the present and future well-being of what has been entrusted to us. Congregants rarely appreciate that they are stewards of the future life of their congregation, and that the next generation of their congregation depends a great deal upon the actions of the current congregation. The greater a congregation's stewardship of its future, the more concerned congregants will be about current reality. If we believe that present or future well-being is challenged in some way, we feel concern. Stewardship, quite properly, gives rise to push motives.

If leaders ignore the motivational power of concern, they are overlooking half of their motivational tools. For example, Bill Hybels apparently used to think that motivating goals were all that was needed to promote change. In his popular 2002 book *Courageous Leadership*, he defined vision as "a picture of the future that produces passion."[4] For Hybels, leaders are to imagine such an appealing vision for the future that the vision alone will motivate people by fostering sufficient desire and anticipation (which he calls passion), which produces all the motivational energy needed to pursue the goal. *Courageous Leadership* puts little emphasis on concerns about current reality as a motivational force. Thankfully, appealing goals can motivate all on their own in a one-sided way, as Hybels suggests, but, unfortunately, not always.

I was attending worship at Willow Creek Community Church near Chicago one evening in the mid-1990s when a new vision for personal spiritual development was being rolled out, complete with resources. It looked like a textbook application of *Courageous Leadership*. A decade later in 2004, a congregation-wide survey showed that Willow Creek was falling dishearteningly short of its hopes for spiritual growth among congregants, despite the program. A compelling vision and good goals, it seemed, were insufficient to generate the hoped-for spiritual change in people. In his 2007 book *Holy Discontent,* Hybels told readers that the situation spawned a question that "bounced around in my brain unanswered for twenty-four long months": "What is it that motivates people to work where they work, volunteer their time to the groups they serve, and donate money to the causes they support?" His two years of reflection resulted in what he called his "break-through" insight:

> The point is, the irresistible attraction to a specific cause that compelled these people to invest joyfully of their time, their money, and their energies always linked back to a single spark of frustration that fueled what is now a raging fire in their souls. . . . You can join God in making what is wrong in the world right! And it all starts with you finding your holy discontent; it begins with you determining what it is that you just can't stand.[5]

Goals and vision are crucial because they speak to people's pull motives, but relying on them alone means leaders will miss the motivational help coming from current concerns. In fact, discontent with current reality tends to motivate more than a compelling vision, because we tend to want to leave what we don't like more than approach what we do like.[6] Push motives, it seems, are generally more influential than pull motives.

The motivational impact of concern can be subtle but still very significant. I once served a large congregation that was extremely task oriented. The leadership team believed that the congregation had a need for more mixing, fellowship, and fun, even though congregants apparently did not perceive this need. Then, an opportunity arose: a member offered his services to cater a chicken barbecue in a local park. This get-together would address what the leaders perceived as a need. Perhaps the experience would strengthen a congregational desire to do such things more often. But the question arose, If we cook it, will they come? Would the enjoyment of a social occasion be sufficient motivation to prompt people to attend? As we thought about our nature as a congregation, the senior minister hit upon an idea: Why not hold the barbecue and call it a fund-raiser? Would that appeal to our congregation and bring them out for a good time? To some degree, financial well-being is a motive for nearly every congregation. So we called the barbecue a fund-raiser. The people came out in droves to support their congregation because of their concern for its well-being, and this activity was viewed as an appropriate way to meet the financial need. Hundreds gathered, and we mixed, chatted, played games, and enjoyed good food. We hung around together until well after dark. It was the most successful social event held by the church in all its history. But people came because they were motivated to accomplish a task: to meet the tangible needs of their church, for which they shared concern, through a fund-raiser. In the years that followed, the barbecue has still been promoted as an annual fund-raiser, but now people come more for the fun and fellowship. The motives of the leaders are not what matter in promoting any kind of change; rather, it is the motives that speak to the concerns of the congregation.

## Pull Motives, Hopes, and Goals

Hopes are where our pull motives reside, and motives are why we want our hopes to be fulfilled. Congregations can hold many hopes, such as "I want our congregation to grow," "Mission is important," or "Young people are the future of our church." Take, for example, a hope that our children will one day have a deep Christian faith. A hope such as this one will evaluate positively specific activities we think will fulfill the hope, such as adopting a new and improved church school curriculum or introducing a new youth program. Hopes, then, prompt the formation of goals, which can fulfill our hopes.

Goals have the ability to concentrate motivation that is loosely and vaguely held in hopes. Think of a magnifying lens that can concentrate sunlight to a dot the size of a pinhead. Goals are like magnifying glasses, concentrating hope's motivational power. A great deal of work has been done over the past three decades to learn how to craft goals so they have greater impact. Here are seven characteristics of a well-crafted goal.

1. *The goal is specific.* Every congregation has at least a vague goal to nurture the faith of its adult members, but how does this goal guide effective action? A specific goal, such as "Establish one new home group this year," provides sufficient definition to direct effort. Goal specificity makes the task more understandable and appear more doable, and this leads to greater motivation.
2. *The goal is high.* Setting a high goal also adds motivational power. Hundreds of studies have shown that the worst goal leaders can set is "Do your best," because people generally will not do their best. Establishing one new home group this year in your congregation may be an easy goal, but what about five new groups? People give their best effort when a challenging—but attainable—goal is set because it incites greater effort.
3. *The goal is immediate.* Goal immediacy also prompts motivation. We all know how effort can increase as a deadline looms near. If the goal is to create five new home groups over a twelve-month period, chances are the degree of effort will not be great at the beginning of the year and will climb toward the end of the year. But what if that goal is broken down into intermediate steps—to create one new group every two months? This creates more goal immediacy and thus more motivation to act.
4. *The goal is necessary.* A well-crafted goal is intended to concentrate the motivational energy of the congregation. This energy can be dissipated by pursuing too many important goals. Consequently, leaders should ensure the congregation will focus on only the necessary goals.

5. *The goal is stated using positive language.* Saying "Our goal is to equal last year's financial success at the fund-raiser" is more motivating than "Our goal is to not make less than the fund-raiser did last year." Framing the goal in positive language is more motivating because it affirms capability beliefs.
6. *The goal reaffirms the congregation's sense of identity.* The more a goal can be described as a natural consequence of the congregation's current culture, the more the goal will be embraced and pursued. Goals presented this way will appear less like a change and more like a natural development of what the congregation believes itself to be.
7. *The motives for the goal are clear.* Every goal has a question attached to it: Why pursue this goal? Every time leaders promote striving for a goal, they must talk about the motives that make attainment of the goal important. The clearer everyone is concerning the motives behind the goal, the more motivating the goal will be.

The more leaders can apply these seven characteristics to their goal, the better the goal will focus and concentrate motivational energy, which is really coming from the motives. Goal-setting theory in motivation psychology has shown that meaningful goals help generate what people need to pursue change: a clear direction that focuses their attention as well as greater effort and persistence in striving for goal attainment.

## Motives, Evaluations, and Attitudes

Motives are not inherently motivating, however. Motives need to be switched on for them to cause us to act, and this comes through attitude formation.[7] The formation process evaluates any idea, object, or behavior with some degree of favor or disfavor. At its most basic level, the evaluation determines that such things—called *attitude objects*—are right or wrong, true or false, good or bad, liked or disliked. For example, you may think the principle that "all men are created equal" is either true or false in actual practice in the United States. That's an attitude. You may think cream soda is delicious or disgusting. That's an attitude. Attitudes are evaluations that convey a sense of favor or disfavor toward the object of the attitude, and they can be the loftiest of ideals or about a soda pop. Now some of our attitude objects are potential motives ("There should be greater equality among people in our country" or "I am thirsty"). Attitude formation related to motives leads to different evaluations: act or don't act, approach or avoid. When the evaluation determines *act*, then the attitude gives motivational energy to the motive ("I will participate in the demonstration at the White House, and I'll take a cream soda with me").

The reason we form attitudes is to create mental shortcuts for decision making. Can you imagine what life would be like if every time you spotted a can of cream soda you had to conduct a full-scale evaluation to determine whether you liked it . . . and then conduct a full-scale diagnostic to determine whether you wanted it? If we operated like this, we wouldn't get past the bathroom in the morning ("Is brushing my teeth for one minute sufficient, or do I need to brush for five minutes?"). To make decision making easier, we form attitudes that become semipermanent decisions we can refer to again and again to do an end run around our need to conduct evaluations.

This doesn't mean, however, that we walk around all day aware of all our attitudes. That awareness would be unwieldy as well. Again, to make life easier, we file attitudes away—out of sight and out of mind. They become latent—but are still ready and available to be called upon and used when needed. But even this can make dealing with attitudes difficult, so we let many attitudes function subconsciously, making decisions for us unawares. Then, to make decision making even easier for us, we let many attitudes function routinely without any supervision. Putting these ideas together, we realize that we have already predecided a lot of our decisions in life and predetermined a lot of our behaviors. Our actions are still motivated, but now we call them habit. Think about this: do you typically make a conscious decision to get out of bed in the morning, or do you just get out of bed?

This way of human functioning is a blessing, truly. Attitudes prevent traffic jams in our head. But they can also be a curse. The reality that attitudes can function latently, subconsciously, and routinely as shortcuts in decision making can preempt thoughtful decision making, which happens all the time in congregations.

Think of a congregation in which the leaders propose, without warning, that the traditional style of worship should be replaced by a contemporary one. There will typically be two groups in the congregation: those who like the idea and those who do not. Some people like traditional worship because they prefer its pageantry and language, they find it makes them feel comfortable and secure, maintaining tradition is for them an important value, and they find pleasure in singing hymns. These are some of the motives behind their preference for a traditional style. Other people like contemporary worship because they enjoy singing the same style of music they listen to on the radio, they prefer an upbeat worship atmosphere to a reverent one, and they believe that contemporary worship will attract the younger generation to church, which is a concern to them. These are some of the motives behind their preference for a contemporary style. For both groups the motives have been evaluated and formed into attitudes toward worship style. It is unlikely that those in either group sat down one day and consciously evaluated these motives. Rather, over time people's experience in worship and their response to their experience was the incubator for their attitudes, forming them slowly and subconsciously into preferences. These preferences, in turn, function like preevaluations and predecisions when those congregational leaders propose, without warning, that the traditional style of worship should be replaced by a contemporary one.

What proportion of the congregation, do you suppose, will hear that proposal, lean back in their pew, and think, "OK, let me reflect on that. Let's hear what the leaders have to say. Let's hear all sides in this discussion and consider the pros and cons. Let me think about my motives and theirs." My hunch is that these folk will be in the small minority. Most people will probably know almost instantly whether the idea is good or bad, one they like or don't like, and whether it is one the congregation should approach or avoid. The mental processes of the majority of congregants will probably make a quick reference to their prevailing attitudes and then make a determination based on that. After all, attitudes are there to expedite decision making. Consequently, people react quickly to the proposal of changing worship styles by thinking yes or no. Attitudes can act as barriers to real consideration of the merits of change.

Studies have shown that this quick referencing to attitudes in decision making potentially leads to other unhelpful consequences as well.[8]
Attitudes—as preevaluations and predecisions—tend to preposition
us to take a side, even before we've begun to think about the issue at
hand, and that preposition can become the starting point for our consideration of a proposed direction. In other words, attitudes bias our
thinking processes. Next, debating a proposal can cause us to defend
our attitudes, which means we may not actually hear, reflect on, and
appreciate the merits of the proposal. Finally, the act of defending attitudes tends to make attitudes more rigid. Many congregational debates
can seem like people are talking past each other—which is exactly what
they are doing. As debate continues, the growing rigidity of attitudes
can lead to real conflict. It can also lead people to form a new attitude:
that those on the other side of the debate have closed minds—which
is not quite correct. What they have are fixed attitudes. The irony is
that the very people who claim others have closed minds have probably contributed in no small measure to closing them through this
cascade of consequences.

We form attitudes as mental shortcuts for decision making, which
works for us most of the time. But as this illustration shows, attitudes
can also work against us. To have a real discussion about the merits
of change, leaders need to help congregants to not let their thinking
be preempted by their attitudes. Instead, leaders need to help people
to reconsider their attitudes. Reconsidering attitudes opens up the
possibility that people can look again at motives and perhaps change
their minds.

Knowing the reality of how attitudes function can make congregational leadership appear daunting. But here is the good news: attitudes
can change. I've been defining them as *semi*permanent decisions.
When attitudes change, then what seemed wrong can now seem right,
dislike can change to like, and avoiding can change to approaching.
Reflecting on motives can lead to these shifts in thinking: diminishing
the priority of some current motives, recognizing the importance of
other motives, and changing the relative influence among motives.
Reevaluating motives can lead to the formation of new attitudes,
which in turn helps us make new choices and encourages movement
in new directions.

The more significant a proposed change appears to people, the more leaders will have to encourage changed attitudes if they wish to effect change. Fortunately, leaders don't need to pursue and overhaul all the attitudes among all the people of their congregation to do this. Leaders need to focus only on the attitudes that may influence specific decisions about the future of the congregation.

## How to Help People Change Their Attitudes

Every individual harbors a collection of motives, and a congregation is a collection of many different individuals. When it comes to considering a vision for the future, people will likely have motives for and against pursuing the proposed direction. The role of leaders is to reduce the influence of motives that stand against the vision (called *resisters*) and increase the influence of motives that encourage pursuit of the vision (called *drivers*). Leaders want to tip the balance of motives in favor of the new vision.

Imagine a teeter-totter with a number of motives sitting on either side of the fulcrum, and the motivational strength of those motives (some motives carry more weight with people than other motives). (See figure 2.1.) Leaders seek to tip the teeter-totter in the direction of pursuing the vision. Leaders will want to do this work before bringing a vision to the congregation for a decision, because attitudes are predecisions and preevaluations. Helping congregants reconsider their attitudes in advance will hopefully increase the number of preevaluations and predecisions that will favor the proposal when it comes time to make the actual formal decision.

Not all change situations are this simple. When a congregation considers a new direction for its future, people can hold a complex mix of attitudes and motives for and against the project. This makes leadership difficult, especially if the overall balance is tipping away from acceptance. Changing attitudes is a three-step process. The following simple scheme will be further developed in the second half of the book.

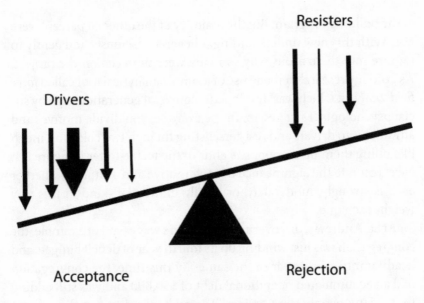

**Figure 2.1 The Balance of Drivers and Resisters**

1. Determine what are the most influential motives and attitudes motivating congregants to pursue a vision for the future (drivers), as well as the motives and attitudes motivating congregants to reject the vision for the future (resisters).
2. Determine what will be required for congregants to consider changing their attitudes through strengthening drivers and diminishing the power of resisters.
3. As much as possible, before presenting a vision for the future, help congregants to reflect on and change their attitudes.

Here's an example of a complicated situation and how the three-step process for changing attitudes was used. Just before I arrived at St. Andrew's Church in 2000, the congregation made a significant decision: to proceed with a $1.2 million facility expansion. I arrived that fall ready to go with fund-raising and construction. In my first weeks there, however, I quickly began to learn something unexpected about my new congregation. It turned out that the 20 percent of members who attended the congregational meeting were substantially in favor of the building program. But the majority of the other 80 percent were not. With this new understanding, I began consciously and gently to inquire into the reasons why so many were not keen on the project. As I did my research, I made use of a simple analytical tool called *force field analysis*, which was developed a couple of generations ago by social psychologist Kurt Lewin. In the exercise, you divide motives and attitudes into drivers and resisters, listing them in two columns, much like piling them up on opposite ends of the teeter-totter in figure 2.1. Next you rate the significance of each motive and attitude—whether each is strongly, moderately, or mildly influential—and in this way weight each one.

At St. Andrew's, discovering the resisters was easy. For example, the congregation was just winding up its fourth year of deficit budgets and heading into a fifth year of the same. By this time, the congregation had an accumulated operational debt of $50,000 and was still adding to it. Many people were saying, "We can't afford to pay the current bills now, so we can't possibly afford a mortgage." Many people took a belief about the congregation's financial well-being ("We can't afford a mortgage") and evaluated it as a motive ("Avoid!"), creating attitudes unfavorable to the project. Consequently, many in the congregation thought the proposed project was foolish. That attitude was a strong resister.

Once the main drivers and resisters are known, leaders determine what will be required for congregants to consider changing their attitudes. An attitude is an evaluation rooted in evidence and a belief about that evidence. In this case the evidence for many people at St. Andrew's came from the monthly updates that the congregation was running in the red. To change their attitude, congregants needed to see congregational finances move into the black, with income exceeding expenses. This would foster a new belief—the congregation is financially healthy—which could be evaluated differently as a motive: "We can afford a mortgage. Approach." If St. Andrew's was to move ahead successfully with the building project, the financial managers of the congregation would have to help the congregation improve its financial situation.

An even bigger concern had to do with the congregation's ability to raise funds. For many people the annual deficits were evidence that the congregation was unwilling to give more money. This view of the congregation's financial stewardship was an attitude. Many believed that the congregation was aging, which made them pessimistic about the future, and therefore they thought additions to the facility may not be needed. This was an attitude. Some people did not see any current need for extra space. This group was predominantly composed of people who came to church only on Sundays for worship and did not see how much midweek activity there was, so they formed their evaluation based on the limited evidence they saw. This was an attitude.

The other side of the teeter-totter held several important motives for building that were drivers for the project. Office space for the current staff was inadequate, and the congregation wanted to add even more staff. We also needed more space for both existing and new midweek activities. There was also a growing community partnership with the YMCA, and we rented space to the organization. Providing more space to the Y would result in more income for the congregation, and this in turn would cover a portion of the mortgage costs. Then, after the mortgage was paid off, we would have this income free and clear. Many motives on the teeter-totter were drivers that would shift the balance of motivation toward building the addition. What needed to happen was this: more congregants needed to understand these drivers and give these motives greater importance in their thinking.

But motivation is not just the result of balancing motives and attitudes. Moderators of motivation can strengthen or weaken motivation, and these can also be added to the force field analysis. For example, when I arrived at St. Andrew's, the congregation had multiple expensive goals. The month before St. Andrew's members decided to build, they also created a new position for an additional minister. The annual salary and benefits for this minister would equal the annual cost of a mortgage. "What is really most important here: the building or the staff?" In addition, the congregation had a few live controversies not associated with the facility expansion goal, but they added background noise and anxiety that detracted from focus on the building project. Finally, many felt little urgency to get on with construction, and a sense of urgency adds to motivation. All these I listed as resisters.

In total, I found twelve reasons why people didn't want to move ahead. I took my findings to the group responsible for leading the building project. They not only grudgingly agreed that what I found were real and substantial issues but they also added an attitude I hadn't even heard about. I led the group in a round of force field analysis of St. Andrew's situation. We considered the drivers and resisters and determined what needed to happen to change the strengths of motives and to change attitudes. We then agreed to put the building initiative on the back burner for eighteen months in order to strengthen people's sense of the drivers and do away with as many of the resisters as possible. I knew that before presenting a vision for the future, the leaders of the congregation needed to help congregants reflect on their attitudes, make new evaluations, and come to hold renewed attitudes.

Over those eighteen months the congregation balanced its budget, showing fiscal responsibility. We set aside the desire for a third minister, making the facility the only major priority. We ran a successful "Miracle Month" campaign to raise $125,000 to install an elevator right away and pay off the accumulated debt. People were surprised and pleased by the quick success of the campaign, which changed attitudes about our ability to raise funds. All the controversies were dealt with, reducing the congregational anxiety that was spilling over onto the building project. At the same time, the building committee carefully recrafted its message regarding the motives for expansion so that it would appeal to a greater portion of the congregation. One of the most respected leaders in the congregation, a chartered accountant who was known to have a cautious nature, stepped in to head up the project. This increased the congregation's trust in its leaders. When he said we could afford to do the project, people believed him. The congregation was made aware that inflation in construction costs in Calgary was annually adding $100,000 to the projected costs, increasing the sense of urgency to act. Finally, the story of this expansion was linked to the stories of St. Andrew's past, showing how our new initiative was simply the next in a series of historic actions our congregation had taken for the sake of a stronger future.

It was only after all this work was accomplished that the leadership team brought the building expansion proposal back to the congregation for consideration. Many attitudes had changed, and congregants now had different preevaluations and predecisions to use in reconsidering the proposal. The congregation widely embraced the project. The groundbreaking was held within the year, and the mortgage was paid off within eight years of construction.

**Motives**
—such as beliefs, values, priorities, feelings,
incentives, personal goals, needs, costs,
and negative outcomes to be avoided—
are considered in an evaluative process, which forms

**Attitudes.**
When attitudes are inclined positively toward
a future goal, they empower the motives that lead to

**Intentions,**
which is a readiness to act.
When people believe that
they can do what they intend, this belief leads to

**Goal Commitment,**
the choice to act on intentions.

**Figure 2.2 The Precursors of Goal Commitment**

Helping people change their attitudes can be very hard. But people can and do change attitudes every day, as illustrated by changing consumer behavior, a person finally choosing to lose weight, growing environmental consciousness, improvements in business ethics, the increasing number of public places where smoking is forbidden, the change in which political party holds an office, and religious conversions. Attitudes can and do change all the time. This gives us hope. How leaders can help change attitudes will be explored in more detail in chapter 6.

## Moving from Motives through Attitudes to Intentions to Act

But changing attitudes is not yet enough to foster real change. There are two more steps in the motivational process: developing intentions and choosing action.

Intention is a person's readiness to act, and it is indicated by statements such as, "I will pursue this goal," "I expect to have this done Tuesday," "I will try," and "We should do this!"[9] Now, people have mixed views about the concept of intentions. Just ask anyone on January 10 how they are doing with their New Year's resolutions. I can also hear some readers thinking, "Intentions are not enough," which is quite right. I also think Prime Minister Margaret Thatcher was correct when she said, "No one would remember the Good Samaritan if he *only* had good intentions."[10] All true. Humans don't always do what they intend, but studies consistently demonstrate that the best predictor of action is first having an intention to act. Studies have also found that intentions as one factor in motivation exerts about 20 to 30 percent of the influence that prompts people to act on their motives.[11] The role of intentions is significant.

But can intentionality lead to congregational change? Church historian Diana Butler Bass found that the answer is yes. From 2002 to 2006, she conducted a Lilly Endowment funded research project on a large number of remarkably vital mainline congregations. These congregations were very different from each other in their histories, community settings, denominational heritage, demographics, and so on. There was also great variety in the activities that were giving these congregations a sense of vitality: worship renewal, spiritual practices, expressing hospitality, engaging in mission, pursuing justice, offering catechesis, and so on. But despite this diversity, they had one thing in common: these congregations had moved from being congregations of habit to being congregations of intention. Bass writes:

> Intentional congregations are marked by mobility, choice, risk, reflexivity, and reflection. They think about what they do and why they do it in relation to their own history, their cultural context, the larger Christian story found in scripture and liturgy, and in line with the longer traditions of the Christian faith. In addition to *thinking* about their practices, they reflexively engage practices that best foster their sense of identity and mission.[12]

When members of a congregation think about "what they do and why they do it," they are acting as stewards of their congregation's life, reconsidering their attitudes and reflecting on their motives. What Bass found were congregations doing the kind of work suggested in this chapter.

When people evaluate motives as important and act, they form attitudes that are motivating. If these attitudes, in turn, are evaluated as having sufficient priority, importance, or urgency, people then form an intention to act based on the attitudes. But as we've noted, intentions are generally not enough. People also need to believe that they are able to do what they intend to do, and that their actions will result in attaining the goal sought in the intention. Figure 2.3 illustrates the process.

Motives to act are evaluated, which forms

Attitudes that give motivational energy to motives.
Attitudes are then evaluated, which forms

Intentions: the readiness to act.

A Goal becomes
the focus of intentions.

Two positive beliefs about the goal
must be present before one acts:

Will this goal          Can I attain
satisfy my motives?          this goal?

Motivated Action occurs if
the answer to both questions is "yes."

**Figure 2.3 The Generation of Motivated Action**

Leaders can foster motivation for change at the point where intentions are formed, just as they can foster motivation at the point of attitude formation. Because attitudes are preevaluations and predecisions, leaders need to influence attitudes *before* the moment of decision. Intention—the readiness to act—is what people consider *at the time of* decision making. Leaders strengthen intentions and help people choose change by affirming

- the motives for the proposed change,
- the attitudes that evaluate the proposal positively,
- the goal as the best way to attain what is hoped for, and
- the ability of the people to attain the goal.

This leadership work takes place through forming and presenting the change message, which is covered in chapters 7 and 8.

## Putting It All Together

The psychological theory covered thus far is portrayed in the comprehensive scheme for understanding motivation shown in figure 2.4.

This chapter has explored the scheme to the point of forming intentions. But intentions are not enough. People must also trust in their ability to achieve what they intend in order to be motivated to act. Trust moderates motivation, making it stronger or weaker. We turn to this topic in the next chapter.

Stewardship
of the congregation's
present and future life
prompts the evaluation of
⇩

Current Reality,
which can create
⇩

Attitudes,
which are evaluations
of how the congregation
is doing.
These attitudes can contain
⇩

Push Motives
that are experienced as
⇩

Concerns,
which motivate a
congregation to form

Hope
for the congregation's
future prompts
creation the of
⇩

Goals, which are
shaped by
⇩

Attitudes,
which are evaluations of
how best to fulfill
congregational hopes.
These attitudes can contain
⇩

Pull Motives
that are experienced as
⇩

Desire and Anticipation,
which motivate a
congregation to form

⇩

Intentions
—a readiness to act—
but to act on intentions a congregation must also
⇩

Trust that the plan is the best pathway to get from
current reality to goal attainment and that the
congregation is able to accomplish the plan.
Trusting that intentions can be achieved fosters
⇩

Goal Commitment,
which is the choice to act on intentions.

**Figure 2.4 A Scheme for Understanding Motivation**

## CHAPTER 3

# Trust at Work:
# The Moderation of Motivation

*Then as it neared the top of the grade that had so discouraged the*
*large engine, it went more slowly but still kept saying, "I think I can,*
*I think I can." It reached the top by dint of brave effort and then*
*went on down the grade beyond, congratulating itself, "I thought I*
*could, I thought I could."*[1]
—Thinking One Can, *later known as* The Little Engine That Could

Stewardship of current reality and hopes for the future mark the two
poles of the here-to-there trajectory for change, and leaders often assume that the push and pull motives arising from these two poles is
sufficient for motivation. But many congregations fail to act despite
the best of intentions because they don't believe they are able to do
what they intend. The motivation coming from push and pull motives
is moderated (either strengthened or weakened) by people's beliefs
about their abilities. Confidence arises from two specific beliefs: first,
*the goal is attainable through the congregation's own efforts,* and second,
*the congregation's context* (its immediate neighborhood or community,
or the broader culture) *will enable it to attain the goal.* We will explore
these two beliefs in turn.

## Capability Beliefs

Do you remember the children's story *The Little Engine That Could*? Many congregations today feel like the great engine that says, "I can't. That is too much a pull for me." The great engine had a debilitating belief, even though the success of the little switch engine shows that the great engine indeed had all the ability it needed. But what held it back? Weak capability beliefs.

In technical terms, capability beliefs are called *perceived efficacy beliefs*,[2] and they are a key factor in producing our sense of competence and prompting human action. According to the preeminent Stanford psychologist Albert Bandura, capability beliefs are a person's beliefs in his or her abilities to organize activity, channel energy, and sustain effort until the activity is completed. The important point here is that they are *perceived* beliefs. They are not about one's actual ability but one's perceptions and evaluations of one's ability. Capability beliefs, then, are attitudes about oneself.

In the first months after he graduated from high school, Elvis Presley visited Sun Records twice to record four songs at his own expense, hoping to be discovered in the process. Discovery did not come. He auditioned as lead singer for two different bands but was turned down. He explained later to his father, "They tell me I can't sing." But Elvis maintained his personal, strong capability beliefs, certain in his own mind that he indeed could sing despite what his world was telling him. The world's opinion changed when he recorded Arthur Crudup's song "That's All Right." The rest, as they say, is history.[3] Elvis's belief that he had an ability to sing moderated his motivation, keeping his motivation strong and sustained until the big break came.

Weak capability beliefs cause people to set low goals for themselves or to avoid some activities altogether. It also leads people to low goal commitment and persistence, causing them to give up quickly if things aren't working out well. Strong capability beliefs, by comparison, tend to prompt people to set challenging goals and encourage persistence in accomplishing goals. People with strong capability beliefs view setbacks as the consequence of a lack of effort rather than a lack of ability, and so they respond by trying harder. These are the people who say to themselves, "I think I can, I think I can!"

Capability beliefs are fostered and strengthened in people through their own self-reflection on their positive experience of doing something. This statement contains three important elements. First, capability beliefs are built through *doing*. The second important element is that the experience of doing should be *positive*. Success in accomplishing things builds positive beliefs about what the congregation can do, while frustrations and failure can do the opposite. But you need more than the positive experience. The third element—*reflection*—integrates the congregation's experience into its sense of self. Reflection is how a congregation learns something about itself from its positive experience of doing, which turns that experience into stronger capability beliefs. When a congregation can tell its story in a way that affirms its ability to rise to the challenge, it can remember and pass on its capability beliefs. When these three elements are worked through, capability beliefs are strengthened and the motivation to take on greater challenges of change can grow.

But what if your congregation has generally weak capability beliefs? What if it is like the great engine that responds to challenges with, "I can't; that is too much a pull for me"? There are a few strategies that can strengthen capability beliefs within a congregation and bolster its sense of confidence when considering new goals. The strongest intervention is to provide the congregation with an *enactive mastery experience*, which is exactly what it says: doing something with the primary purpose of experiencing success so that the congregation will have a greater sense of mastery. Leaders do this by encouraging the congregation to take on a challenge that it will have to step up for, but not too far up. When the congregation reflects on its successful experience achieving the goal, overcoming obstacles, and persevering until the conclusion, the experience can have a positive effect on the capability beliefs of the congregation. This, in turn, can cause people to believe that they can do even more the next time they are challenged. A leader can use enactive mastery experiences to prepare the way for a bigger, more important challenge.

An example: I was once invited to consult with a congregation to help members do some planning. In discussing the prospects for the congregational workshop with the leaders, I came to appreciate a few things about the congregation. It had not engaged in any kind of strategic planning in living memory. Members knew they had many challenges before them that seemed overwhelming—too overwhelming to even tackle. The idea of setting some goals to address any of the challenges was highly intimidating to them. So I suggested that they could aim for three or four goals that were relatively modest and could be accomplished relatively quickly. The leaders agreed. At the workshop the congregation's conversation revolved around members' concern for the future and their desire to attract young families. Their hope was evident, but so too was their belief that they couldn't attain their goal. They had low capability beliefs. So instead of addressing their issue in a substantial way, we explored things the congregation could do and realistically achieve quickly that would get them headed in the right direction. First, congregants agreed to give their nursery a complete renovation to make it look appealing—a fun and safe place. Second, two young mothers agreed to create a weekly moms-and-tots group and to invite their friends to attend. A few older women volunteered to provide snacks and beverages weekly, as well as to act as sitters for the children, so that the moms could just drop in and enjoy the social time. Everyone agreed that a six-month timeline for both projects was realistic. After these two goals were achieved, the congregation wanted to adopt some bolder goals for their future. Sometimes a congregation needs to take a smaller, preliminary step before it takes a significant leap.

A second strategy for building capability beliefs is through a *vicarious experience of mastery*, which is to observe, learn from, and draw confidence from the experience of others doing what you want to do. Think back to the story of the little engine that could. The large engine looked at the long train of freight cars and concluded initially, "That is too much a pull for me." But how would that same large engine feel after watching the little switch engine pull the long train up the hill? The large engine would say, "Well, if that little switch engine can do it, then I can do it!" This is a vicarious experience of mastery. This is to learn from—and draw confidence from—someone else who has done what you wish to accomplish.

A vicarious mastery experience is most helpful if your congregation has very little positive or negative experience of its own in the challenge it is considering. Draw the attention of congregants to another congregation that once looked like your congregation and achieved what your congregation desires to do. The things you want to learn from the model congregation include the following:

- Why did they want to make these changes? In other words, what were their motives? Are the motives of your congregation like those of the model congregation?
- How did they plan to move from their current reality to their desired goal?
- What obstacles did they deal with, and how?
- What helped them persevere until they attained their goal?
- What did they learn through experience that could make it easier for your congregation to do the same thing?
- How is their life better now because they made the change?
- What other congregations have made the same change, and how are they doing today?

Listen to the answers to these questions with an ear to the motivations of the model congregation. In reflecting on a vicarious experience, the idea is not simply for you to learn the nuts and bolts of making the proposed change. It is also to lean upon and draw from their sense of strengthened capability beliefs so that your congregation can gain more confidence to do what that congregation did.

An example of this strategy comes from a Presbyterian congregation in southern Ontario that had been slowly but steadily growing in size. In the early 1990s the leaders of the congregation began to yearn for a breakthrough in faithfulness, vitality, and size. So the leaders began to look for a congregation that already looked like what they wanted to become, a model to emulate. Like many other churches in North America, the congregation they chose as their model was Willow Creek. St. Andrew's studied it, read its publications, and sent people to its workshops. And they worked hard at it. Today they are the second largest congregation in the Presbyterian Church in Canada. But the point of my story is what happened next. St. Andrew's became a popular host for leadership conferences among Presbyterians. Many established congregations looked at St. Andrew's and said to themselves, "They used to look just like us, and see what they've been able to do. Let's learn more. If they could do it, then maybe we can do it." St. Andrew's has had an important ministry to other churches as it has shared its positive experience of change. Vicarious learning allows a congregation to gain a sense of mastery by drawing on the experience of another congregation.

A third strategy, *persuasion*, is secondary to and supports the first two. It helps people reflect on their attitudes about their capability beliefs. Persuasion provides congregants with information that offers evidence of the congregation's capability. When that evidence comes from a person congregants trust, then people usually consider it credible. Once a congregation has had an enactive mastery experience, persuasion helps congregants reflect on their positive experience of doing, which can lead to stronger capability beliefs. Similarly, persuasion helps congregants integrate their vicarious learning from other model congregations with their beliefs about their own congregation. This also leads to stronger capability beliefs.

Capability beliefs can be strengthened through a number of smaller interventions as well:

- celebrating accomplishments and expressing gratitude
- drawing confidence from unrelated past experiences and directing it toward the new challenge
- clarifying goals so that congregants have a better guide for assessing their capability for attainment
- reducing distractions by limiting the number of concurrent goals

Over time the congregation's experience of successfully attaining goals can build a general sense of capability belief that has an impact on any aspect of its life and mission. Any effort by leaders to strengthen the capability beliefs will always pay dividends in the long run.

## Context Beliefs

Simply believing in our abilities will not always carry the day. Everything we do has a context. A congregation's context is found beyond its walls, and can be as immediate as the street the building sits on, the congregation's local neighborhood, the town or city in which it is located, or the culture of the surrounding society. A congregation will act, or not act, depending upon what members believe about their context. An enthusiastic and gifted Chinese pastor may not feel very motivated to establish the Mandarin-language congregation he dreams of founding if he believes the number of Chinese immigrants in his community is negligible. A congregation will not reach out to its neighborhood if it believes people simply aren't interested in going to church anymore. A congregation may have strong capability beliefs ("I think I can!"), but if it does not also believe that its environment will respond to its efforts, it probably won't even try. At a minimum, congregants need to believe that their context will not present an insurmountable barrier to success. In other words, a congregation has to believe "We are able!" and "Our context makes it possible." Technically, context beliefs are called *locus of control beliefs*. Locus of control is said to be internal if people believe they are masters of their own destiny. Consequently, hope will be strengthened. Locus of control is said to be external if people believe they are victims of their situation. As a result, hope will be weakened.

Say a chemist invents new glue that is not very sticky and never really dries to a permanent bond. He's excited by his finding and the prospect of it becoming the next big thing in the world of adhesives. His boss, however, might tell him that no one wants glue that doesn't glue things together. The context belief of the boss, then, could prevent the development of this glue into a product . . . unless someone identified a market for a glue that doesn't glue well. The company 3M has sold tons of this kind of glue. Have you ever used a Post-it note? After he concocted his low-tack glue in 1968, Spencer Silver spent five years casting about for a possible use. Finally, a colleague at 3M suggested it might be useful for temporarily affixing bookmarks in his hymnbook. Silver's strong positive context beliefs kept him looking for a use for his glue long after most of us would have given up. His strong context beliefs maintained his hope, keeping him motivated until he could turn his invention into a marketable product.

It is my hunch that many congregations have weak context beliefs. Over the past half century, congregations—especially in mainline denominations—have seen their influence and size decline to the point that many congregations view themselves as victims of their changing world rather than shapers of it. Weak context beliefs will diminish motivation for any goal that depends even somewhat on the congregation's context. The greater the number of congregants holding strong context beliefs—that they can overcome any barriers presented by their context—the stronger will be their motivation to attain a goal.

For example, I once worked with a congregation that had a desire to attract new, younger families but saw the dream as pointless. The church had been founded a generation earlier when the whole neighborhood was brand new, at that time composed almost exclusively of young families. Now, thirty years later, the members' perception was that their neighborhood had aged naturally and was still filled with the original homeowners, who were now all older empty nesters. In essence they believed there were no next-generation homeowners and no new young families in the neighborhood. The congregation overall had weak context beliefs, which demotivated them. As I listened to them describe their take on reality, I suddenly recalled a simple observation I had of their neighborhood. "Well, if this is true," I asked, "why does the public school one block away have at least half a dozen portable classrooms in its backyard? If a neighborhood was experiencing a decline in school-aged children, why would the school be adding classrooms?" This observation caught them off guard, and when they thought about it they too recalled the large number of portable classrooms there. One person spoke what most people were thinking: "Maybe there are more young families in our neighborhood than we assume there are." As a result of this discussion, the congregation examined census data for its neighborhood and contacted a local real estate agent to make some inquiries. It turned out that the original homeowners—now retiring and living in homes larger than they needed—were selling their properties to the second generation of homeowners in the neighborhood. In fact, the neighborhood was developing a reputation for being a neighborhood of choice for young families, especially because of the schools. This congregation's assumptions about its neighborhood were challenged and changed by contrary evidence, which in turn changed attitudes. Its epiphany strengthened its context beliefs. In time, congregational efforts to attract new younger families had some success, which in turn strengthened not only its context beliefs ("Our context does enable growth") but also its capability beliefs ("We are able to make growth possible").

Like capability beliefs, context beliefs can be altered by mastery experiences. Members of a congregation can believe their context will impede fulfillment of their hopes and dreams. The congregation might still be persuaded, however, to try an experiment to test the validity of their belief. Instead of striving for the big dream they desire—and think they can't achieve—congregants may agree to a smaller-scale foray in that direction. Some years ago I was a church planter in Canada's retirement capital, Victoria, British Columbia. In the initial months, many in our congregation thought it was pointless to give any effort to attracting young families. After all, this was Victoria, land of the senior citizen! Despite this attitude, the congregation was open to one five-day effort to try to attract young families by holding a vacation Bible school. We rented a large circus tent so that we could hold the VBS on our church property (we didn't have a building). We rented portable toilets. One of our families loaned us their RV to be our kitchen for the week. In the end thirty children who were not a part of our congregation attended the program. The congregation was thrilled! But more than that, their context beliefs were strengthened, which served them well as they took on more initiatives to appeal to younger families.

Also like capability beliefs, context beliefs can be improved through vicarious mastery. If members of your congregation believe their goals are unattainable because the context will impede them, then look for another congregation or two that share your context but were able to attain the same aspiration. Talk to the people in these congregations and learn from them. You might also be able to benefit in a similar way by contracting with a consultant (aka, "an expert") who can open the eyes of your congregation to the possibilities of your context.

## Feedback

Feedback is always produced as a consequence of goal striving. As the congregation implements the plan, the goal provides the standard by which success is judged. The goal is the destination, plan implementation is the path to the destination, and feedback keeps you on track. How many congregations have used a poster with a thermometer to goal into a series of more proximal subgoals creates and maintains a greater sense of urgency. Establishing a trust fund, then, could have as subgoals: finalizing the fund's legal parameters in year one, soliciting three frontrunner donors to seed the fund in year two, conducting initial promotion in year three, reaching 10 percent of the goal by year four, and so on. Breaking down large, distant goals in this way will create understandable and acceptable levels of urgency to ensure progress is maintained.

## Task Complexity

The last car I owned that I could service myself was my 1984 Toyota. Since then modern engineering, emission controls, and computerized components have turned the engine compartment of my vehicles into a mind-boggling puzzle of metal and plastics. I have tried twice with my current automobile to change the air filter and failed to figure it out both times. Maintaining a car is no longer straightforward. Now, I could learn how to maintain my own car, but it would take so much time and effort. The grief entailed in figuring it all out myself is simply too high for me. Consequently, I let an expert do it for me.

Increasing task complexity decreases motivation. Our inclination to pursue a goal increases when the strategy is understandable and seems doable. But not everything we want to do is straightforward. A pastor told me his small congregation sees newcomers visit but never stay to become members. As I helped him analyze the situation, we came to see that the congregation needed to learn how to adopt new people into their faith family in much the same way as a nuclear family adopts a new child into its midst. The more we talked about this, the more we realized how many aspects of the congregation's life would need to change to facilitate this kind of adoption. "I have no idea how we could do that" was the pastor's honest answer. His hesitation was understandable, for despite the fact that the goal of growth sounded straightforward, accomplishing it was complex. It would mean presenting a new image of the congregation to the wider community, fostering new habits of hospitality, as well as instituting cultural changes to help congregants enjoy opening up their current circles of friendship to include strangers. Just thinking about effecting this much change

Like capability beliefs, context beliefs can be altered by mastery experiences. Members of a congregation can believe their context will impede fulfillment of their hopes and dreams. The congregation might still be persuaded, however, to try an experiment to test the validity of their belief. Instead of striving for the big dream they desire—and think they can't achieve—congregants may agree to a smaller-scale foray in that direction. Some years ago I was a church planter in Canada's retirement capital, Victoria, British Columbia. In the initial months, many in our congregation thought it was pointless to give any effort to attracting young families. After all, this was Victoria, land of the senior citizen! Despite this attitude, the congregation was open to one five-day effort to try to attract young families by holding a vacation Bible school. We rented a large circus tent so that we could hold the VBS on our church property (we didn't have a building). We rented portable toilets. One of our families loaned us their RV to be our kitchen for the week. In the end thirty children who were not a part of our congregation attended the program. The congregation was thrilled! But more than that, their context beliefs were strengthened, which served them well as they took on more initiatives to appeal to younger families.

Also like capability beliefs, context beliefs can be improved through vicarious mastery. If members of your congregation believe their goals are unattainable because the context will impede them, then look for another congregation or two that share your context but were able to attain the same aspiration. Talk to the people in these congregations and learn from them. You might also be able to benefit in a similar way by contracting with a consultant (aka, "an expert") who can open the eyes of your congregation to the possibilities of your context.

## Feedback

Feedback is always produced as a consequence of goal striving. As the congregation implements the plan, the goal provides the standard by which success is judged. The goal is the destination, plan implementation is the path to the destination, and feedback keeps you on track. How many congregations have used a poster with a thermometer to show progress toward a fund-raising goal? The changing "temperature" on the poster is feedback. In general, goal setting and feedback are two peas from the same pod: each one needs the other. Goals are useless without some way to assess whether you are closing in on them. Feedback is useless unless there is some meaningful standard to judge progress against.

But feedback is also a powerful mechanism to maintain motivated activity because it easily affects capability and context beliefs. Let's say the progress in the fund-raising campaign is going much more slowly than expected. Congregants can develop a weak context belief that says, "This recession is holding people back from supporting the campaign." People can also adopt a weak capability belief that says, "Our people can't afford to support this cause right now." Slow progress can even lead a congregation to develop a negative sense of self, such as, "The people here just don't care about their church." Low capability and context beliefs and pessimistic narrative scripts will all moderate motivation by reducing it. Feedback like this is experienced as discouragement.

Discouragement can have several results. It can make people question whether the goal is too lofty, prompting them to lower the goal. Discouragement can deplete the sense of willpower needed to continue on the project. It can also nudge people to focus on other activities in order to distract themselves from the discouraging one. It can push people to discount the feedback, which will dispel their feelings of discouragement. These responses help people sidestep negative feedback, but sidestepping removes the course-correcting role feedback has in goal attainment. The role of leaders, then, is not to avoid negative feedback per se, but rather to help people not feel discouraged by it. How to make feedback useful will be explored in depth in chapter 10.

## Other Moderators of Motivation

So far we've looked at the major role of context and capability beliefs, as well as feedback in moderating motivation. Beyond these major players, several small players also can contribute to strengthening motivation.

## Urgency and Deadlines

Urgency reflects a goal's relative importance and its attainment deadline, creating a sense of priority that in turn strengthens motivation. Everyone who has ever been a student knows the motivational power of urgency. A student's reaction will be different depending on whether the instructor tells her that the ten-page paper is due in two months or in two days, and on whether the paper is worth 5 percent or 95 percent of her final mark. Distant goals and goals of little consequence do not motivate people as much as proximal and critical goals. This is such an important moderator of motivation that Harvard business professor John Kotter names "establishing a sense of urgency" as the first step in his eight-stage change process.[4] Indeed, some business leadership books take creating urgency so seriously that they suggest CEOs consider artificially manipulating a sense of urgency by allowing sales or shareholder profits to fall in order to motivate their workforce to change out of anxiousness. Other books suggest that CEOs cast the company's current business practices in such an unfavorable light compared with the competition that they create a "burning platform." This essential message is "If we don't change what we are doing now, our relevance and sales (the platform) will burn up, and this company will fold."

Urgency does moderate motivation, but we must take two cautions from human nature. First, people are not stupid. If the sense of urgency is artificial, then many people will see through it and find their motivation declining and cynicism rising. It will also cause diminished trust in the leaders. Second, people may not catch the sense of urgency. For example, many North American congregations and denominations (especially mainline ones) have experienced serious escalating membership decline since the mid-1960s. Despite the basic threat to survival decline creates, many congregations do not see their situation as urgent until they can't pay the bills. Urgency is in the eyes of the beholder.

But if a case for urgency can be made, then it should be made, because it will strengthen motivation. The same thing applies to deadlines as well. If a congregation sets a goal to establish a $5 million endowment fund within twenty years' time, effort to promote the fund may languish until year seven or eight. Breaking down a significant distant goal into a series of more proximal subgoals creates and maintains a greater sense of urgency. Establishing a trust fund, then, could have as subgoals: finalizing the fund's legal parameters in year one, soliciting three frontrunner donors to seed the fund in year two, conducting initial promotion in year three, reaching 10 percent of the goal by year four, and so on. Breaking down large, distant goals in this way will create understandable and acceptable levels of urgency to ensure progress is maintained.

## Task Complexity

The last car I owned that I could service myself was my 1984 Toyota. Since then modern engineering, emission controls, and computerized components have turned the engine compartment of my vehicles into a mind-boggling puzzle of metal and plastics. I have tried twice with my current automobile to change the air filter and failed to figure it out both times. Maintaining a car is no longer straightforward. Now, I could learn how to maintain my own car, but it would take so much time and effort. The grief entailed in figuring it all out myself is simply too high for me. Consequently, I let an expert do it for me.

Increasing task complexity decreases motivation. Our inclination to pursue a goal increases when the strategy is understandable and seems doable. But not everything we want to do is straightforward. A pastor told me his small congregation sees newcomers visit but never stay to become members. As I helped him analyze the situation, we came to see that the congregation needed to learn how to adopt new people into their faith family in much the same way as a nuclear family adopts a new child into its midst. The more we talked about this, the more we realized how many aspects of the congregation's life would need to change to facilitate this kind of adoption. "I have no idea how we could do that" was the pastor's honest answer. His hesitation was understandable, for despite the fact that the goal of growth sounded straightforward, accomplishing it was complex. It would mean presenting a new image of the congregation to the wider community, fostering new habits of hospitality, as well as instituting cultural changes to help congregants enjoy opening up their current circles of friendship to include strangers. Just thinking about effecting this much change

These four values promote an atmosphere of cooperation while discerning a direction for the future, and ultimately help the minority accept the majority view once a direction is chosen.

In writing of procedural fairness Latham asserts, "The importance of justice principles on motivation [in an organization] cannot be over-emphasized."[6] In this statement Latham is speaking primarily about the business environment, but concern for justice is even more important to Christians, who hold justice as such a central value. But while congregations may challenge the unjust behavior of institutions of society, those same congregations are not always aware of their own unjust behavior in managing change. One cannot count the number of congregations and denominations that have been divided because of the lack of sensitivity to procedural fairness when faced with a difficult decision.

## Organizational Commitment

The general degree of commitment people have for their congregation moderates motivation. This is a characteristic of all congregations, although the proportion of members who have high or low commitment to their congregation varies from church to church. Ever since Dean Kelley's 1972 book *Why Conservative Churches Are Growing* was published, church leaders and sociologists have had a great interest in what makes for and builds higher commitment in congregations. The reality is that there is very little leaders can do to improve commitment immediately preceding a change initiative. The degree of organizational commitment as it is will have its impact, and leaders must simply be aware of what congregants' current commitment to their church is and plan around it. Surprises may be in store if leaders don't.

For example, an evangelical congregation was established in Calgary in 1994 following the example of Saddleback Church, Lake Forest, California. The congregation was highly successful, due largely to its appreciation of and response to the consumer mindset of the people it was targeting: adults in their twenties, thirties, and forties. In worship style, programs, and overall ethos, this congregation was tailored for their needs and preferences. As the congregation grew, it moved from one rented facility to another to cope with its increasing size. Finally, when worship attendance was approaching one thousand people on Sunday, the leaders determined that it was time to buy land and prepare to build a facility. They ran a financial campaign, but were disappointed by the poor response. One staff person privately confessed to me, "It never occurred to us when we designed a congregation for a consumer-minded public that we would end up with a congregation of consumers." The financial campaign asked more of this congregation than members, based on their overall commitment, were willing to give. The blow to the congregation's capability beliefs—the sense that "we can do this"—was substantial. Once challenged by this negative experience, the leaders were unwilling to bring the idea of buying property before the congregation again until some time had passed. The good news is that this congregation continues to grow and thrive, and did eventually purchase property for its future facility. Sensitivity regarding congregational commitment is needed before initiating big ideas. But an unfortunate truth is that congregational commitment often can be assessed only through the reaction to such initiatives.

## Remembering God Is Our Ground for Hope

Finally, capability and context beliefs can be strengthened by the trust that God will be "a very present help" (Ps. 46:1) in a time of change. Paul wrote to the Philippian church, "I can do all things through him who strengthens me" (Phil. 4:13), which expresses the belief that our capability is increased because we have God's help. The same assurance can strengthen context beliefs. As we read in Psalm 18, "By you I can crush a troop, and by my God I can leap over a wall. This God—his way is perfect; the promise of the LORD proves true; he is a shield for all who take refuge in him" (vv. 29–30). Trust in God is part of our ground for hope, and this trust reduces the degree of perceived risk always connoted by change.

In some congregations, it is rare to hear talk of relying on God's help when pursuing change, as if these congregations are functionally agnostic. But if the leaders can echo these voices from Scripture—that

God will enhance our capabilities and reduce the barriers in our context—then leaders will be helping congregants tap into their core beliefs, strengthening their sense that "if God is for us, then who [whether ourselves or others] is against us?" (Rom. 8:31).

Some Christians are on the other end of the spectrum. They think that placing trust in anything other than God shows a lack of faith. We need only turn to the parable of the talents to see the importance of trusting in our own abilities as we fulfill the work that we do alongside God. With his master gone and unable to help, the third steward could rely only on himself—which he didn't—and his weak capability beliefs caused him to bury his talent in the ground. He did not trust himself to increase the wealth entrusted to him. The master apparently appreciated this quality in the third steward, and consequently gave this steward only one talent, which was less than he gave to the other two stewards. But here is the point to notice: the master still gave this steward one talent to manage. This act was a sign that the master believed in the steward's ability, even if the steward did not. The trust of the master should have strengthened the steward's capability beliefs.

I believe that behind this parable is the recognition that Christians need to trust in ourselves—trust in our own capabilities. God, after all, has entrusted the work of God's kingdom to our hands. Christ is the master who has gone away and will return, and in the meantime it is our calling to go about his work. And if Christ trusts us to share his work with us, it means that he believes we are able and also believes that the context will not be insurmountable for us. It's an extraordinary idea: God believes in us. This should boost our confidence to be God's coworkers as we go about building on the talents that have been entrusted to us.

## CHAPTER 4

# Motivation-Based Change: Leading with People in Mind

*Leadership means influencing the community to face its problems.*[1]
*—Ronald Heifetz*

Motivating leaders seek to influence the motives people have, the priority people give to their motives, the attitudes people have toward a proposal, the intentions for change people hold, as well as people's beliefs in their ability to effect a proposed change. The next question we will explore is, *when* does the leader do *what*? The answer is shaped by how people generally experience a process of change.

We know that the experience of change can be hard. Congregations commonly find change to be challenging and intimidating, and congregants can find themselves angered and demoralized by their forays into the world of change. This is difficult work. A denominational executive I know contacted one of the most respected congregational consultants of our age. He asked the consultant, "What is the most effective way to bring change in a congregation?" The consultant's answer was swift yet sincere and sympathetic: "Start a new congregation."

Change can be hard for every kind of organization. As Peter Senge and colleagues stated in their book *The Dance of Change*, "Most change initiatives fail."[2] He did not make this claim lightly. Studies by consulting firms Arthur D. Little and McKinsey and Company have shown that two-thirds of Total Quality Management change initiatives failed to produce the hoped-for results. The failure rate of organizational reengineering was in the 70 percent range. Similarly, 75 percent of the mergers of two companies do not bring forth the hoped-for results.[3] Senge concluded his survey with these words: "Clearly, businesses do not have a very good track record in sustaining significant change. There is little to suggest that schools, healthcare institutions, governmental, and non-profit institutions fare any better."[4] Change is not just a church dilemma. It is a human organization dilemma. And yet, as organizations, change we must if we are to thrive.

There are about as many different models for organizational change as there are authors who write about them. What most of these models have in common is that they are schemes to help leaders work logically and progressively through managed change. Now, there is no question that having a tool such as this in a leader's toolbox is invaluable (I will be proposing one shortly), but these schemes tend to have significant limitations. First, most models for organizational change are crafted to meet the needs of the leaders in managing change rather than the needs of people in the organization who are experiencing the change. Second, most models presume that an organization is an amorphous group rather than being a collection of individuals. I find it interesting that an idea popular among leadership writers is that their models can help the leader *drive* change. This word causes me to think of cowboys maneuvering cattle from one place to the next, which implies that the people in an organization are a herd. But when we stop to think about it, we realize that an organization changes only to the degree that its individual members change.

The approach to organizational change assumed in this book focuses instead on the needs of the individuals of a congregation, with the assumption that organizational change occurs as a result of the collective change made by many individuals, all moving in the same direction. This assumption implies that it is more useful to begin with models for change that help us understand how people subjectively experience change. We will consider two such models—one for individual change and one for a group of individuals experiencing change.

# A Model for Individual Change:
## The Transtheoretical Model

James Prochaska is a professor of clinical psychology at the University of Rhode Island. As the director of the Cancer Prevention Research Center there, Prochaska is interested in health promotion. Three decades ago he was looking for a way to understand how individuals bring themselves to the point where they will engage in positive self-change. Prochaska, along with clinical psychologist Carlo DiClemente at the University of Maryland, reviewed eighteen major psychotherapy and behavioral change theories, synthesizing them into one umbrella theory that incorporated the common elements of all of them (thus the name *transtheoretical*). They published their first paper on their model in 1983, showing the model's application to people trying to break the smoking habit.[5] Since then the transtheoretical model has become widely used by a variety of medical practitioners to help individuals improve their compliance in taking their medications, deal with addictions, and develop healthy habits. The widespread acceptance of this theory in the health sciences has helped the model find use and acceptance in areas as diverse as addiction counseling, human resource management, consciousness raising concerning social issues, sports coaching, and organizational behavior. According to the transtheoretical model, individuals move through five successive stages of change: precontemplation, contemplation, preparation, action, and maintenance.

## Stage 1: Precontemplation

In the precontemplation stage individuals are unaware of their situation; they don't perceive any problems or contemplate change. Precontemplation is a state of benign ignorance. This is because people's sense of reality, their perspective, their frame of reference or worldview prevents them from seeing otherwise. A proposal for change made to people in the precontemplation stage is typically met by disbelief, disagreement, apathy, defensiveness, or resistance. If individuals assess the pros and cons of a potential change at this point, typically they will believe that the cons outweigh the pros. This is because proposals for change often are based on a different sense of reality, perspective, frame of reference, or worldview. The larger the gap between the person's frame of reference and the frame of reference underlying a new proposal, the more likely the proposal and its rationale will not be understood or acted upon. For people to begin to contemplate change, a proposal needs to be presented in a way that people can understand and appreciate from their current frame of reference. Leaders help congregants shift from precontemplation to contemplation by disconfirming beliefs congregants hold about their current reality and helping them understand the costs of personal inertia, both of which give congregants something to *contemplate*.

## Stage 2: Contemplation

In contemplation individuals have become aware of issues that need to be addressed. Contemplation is a learning phase often marked by the struggle to understand the real nature of the issue, why change may be important and meaningful, and how change might realistically take place. This stage can be a struggle because individuals find that their sense of reality has been challenged, which means they are often called to develop a new sense of reality, perspective, frame of reference, or worldview. This kind of reflection takes people on a journey into a territory unfamiliar to them. Progress in this stage can become stalled due to procrastination, which people use at times as a way to deal with the insecurity and discomfort inherent in this stage. While precontemplation is mostly about learning *what* is really happening, the contemplation stage is more about helping people appreciate *why* it is happening and *how* the situation can be dealt with. Here people will begin to do the cost-benefit analysis of change through their changing perspective, frame of reference, or worldview, weighing the pros against the cons for change. Prochaska asserts that movement to the next stage takes place only when the "decisional balance" favors the pros over the cons. When this happens, individuals develop an intention to adopt change.

## Stage 3: Preparation

The intention to act, however, is still not a complete commitment to act. People who know they must change are not always sure they are capable of changing. From the perspective of organizations, preparation is the stage when strategies for change are chosen and plans created. In motivation terms, this is the stage that strengthens capability and context beliefs. The organizational and the motivational aspects of this stage are related because one influences the other. When people are convinced that the chosen strategy for change will work, they come to believe that "we can do this!" which in turn strengthens goal commitment.

## Stage 4: Action

The action stage is when individuals try new behaviors. People need the greatest motivation at this point, because this phase takes the most time, energy, and effort. Because people in this stage often encounter difficulties breaking old habits, they can find themselves reverting to past behaviors. Indeed, according to the transtheoretical model, people at any time can revert from any stage back to any previous stage. Also, at any stage, people can simply quit the change process. This is highly frustrating and demoralizing for leaders who too often assume upon the first or second reversion that change is impossible. These relapses to the old ways, however, can be interpreted by leaders as learning experiences that can provide them with vital clues for improving action.

## Stage 5: Maintenance

Most individuals eventually adopt a new practice. In maintenance the new practice is now the habit of people. In this stage people work to consolidate the gains they have made and prevent relapses into old ways. The maintenance stage is thus a phase of active work that ends once new habits are sufficiently in place so that the threat of relapse has vanished.

# The Transtheoretical Model
# and Motivation Psychology

The transtheoretical model was designed to describe how individuals subjectively experience personal change. But viewed from a different perspective, Prochaska's model also depicts change as a gradual process of becoming more motivated. Consequently, in recent years different aspects of motivation psychology have been grafted into this model quite successfully and helpfully. The contemplation stage is when people make changes in their sense of reality, perspective, frame of reference, or worldview. This requires reflection on one's attitudes. Studies have shown that attitude change takes place most substantially in the shift from the precontemplation to the contemplation stage.[6] Attitude change continues to take place—but to lesser degrees—in each subsequent stage. This means leaders need to influence attitude change earlier rather than later in the change process.

The contemplation stage is the time when people consider the pros and cons of change as people seek what Prochaska calls a *decisional balance*. What people are really thinking about here are their motives and attitudes, weighing what Lewin calls the drivers and resisters for change. When drivers (pros) outweigh resisters (cons), individuals come to an intention to change, which shifts them from the contemplation stage to the preparation stage. The transtheoretical model states that people shift from the contemplation to the preparation stage when people develop intentions to change, which come from the cumulative influence of attitudes.

Similarly, Bandura's concept of personal efficacy beliefs (what I call capability beliefs) has been integrated with this model. Studies have shown that individuals considering personal change often have weak capability beliefs in the precontemplation stage, and that capability beliefs grow gradually stronger through the contemplation and preparation stages.[7] Individuals shift into the action stage when they hold their capability beliefs with sufficient strength that they feel confident enough to act on their intentions. For leaders this means the preparation stage has to be more than a time for planning. Leaders at this time also need to focus on strengthening the capability and context beliefs of congregants.

In hindsight it would appear that Prochaska's description of the subjective experience of change inadvertently describes individual change as a process of developing motivation for change. More important is that integration allows us to answer the question, *when* does the leader do *what*? Put most simply, addressing attitude change best happens before goals and visions are discussed, and addressing capability and context beliefs best happens after goals and visions are conceived.

The transtheoretical model is also helpful because it is realistic. It acknowledges that the time individuals spend in any one stage will differ. It acknowledges that individuals can become stuck in a particular stage. It also acknowledges that people can regress—more than once—to stages they have already passed through. Anyone who has tried to quit smoking, reduce their weight, or break some bad habit appreciates this from their own personal experience. These observations encourage us to accept one reality of congregational change: not all congregants will appreciate the need for change, develop intentions for change, and engage in change in the same ways or at the same time as others. People are not a herd that leaders can drive through change, so leaders also need a credible theory that describes what happens in a group as individuals adopt change at different times. One such model is diffusion theory.

## A Model for Group Change: Diffusion of Innovations Theory

Sociologist Everett Rogers described how different people in a group will adopt a new idea at different times along a timeline of change, and adopt it for different reasons. Rogers was interested in how an innovation spreads through a group or a society,[8] gaining popularity and adoption over time. Facebook is a good example of the phenomena Rogers was interested in. I remember the first time I learned about the existence of Facebook, which was when my two sons started to use it in high school around 2007.

Introduced in February 2004, Facebook was initially operated only for the benefit of university and high school students and a select number of commercial companies. It was made available to the general public in September 2007, but the growth rate of new users in the following year was no different from the previous year, despite the fact that the number of *potential* users had increased dramatically. (See figure 4.1.) Usage began to take off around the summer of 2008. The number of subscribers doubled to 200 million by April 2009, and doubled again to 400 million by February 2010. According to Checkfacebook.com, by July 2012 the social networking site had more than 868 million active users. Everett Rogers was interested in phenomena like this.

The first seed for his theory actually came from his own childhood experience.[9] Growing up among Iowa corn farmers in the 1930s and '40s, Rogers had noticed how a few specific farmers always seemed to be at the cutting edge of new farming practices, such as the use of hybrid corn seed. Rogers in time labeled such people *innovators*. Innovators are constantly scanning for what they believe will be the next

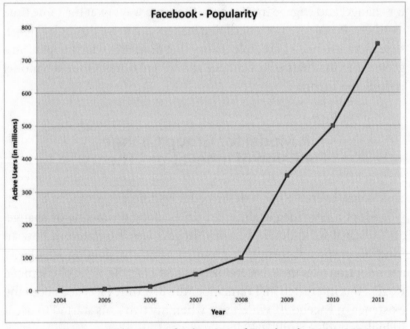

**Figure 4.1 The Rate of Adoption of Facebook, 2004–2011**

Graph obtained from http://en.wikipedia.org/wiki/File:Facebook_popularity.PNG, and used with permission.

improvement, and they are entrepreneurial in capitalizing on improvements. They love new ideas, can cope with a high degree of uncertainty in adopting a new idea, and are willing to accept the reality that not all ideas pan out as hoped. Innovators have a high tolerance for risk.

Around these farmers were some others who liked new ideas but didn't spend their time looking for them. But when they saw a new idea being used by an innovative neighbor, this second group of farmers would quickly recognize obvious advantages and be motivated to adopt the innovation. This group is called the *early adopters*. Early adopters have a fairly high tolerance for risk. They tend to be less dogmatic and more pragmatic compared to those in the later adopter categories. They have better skills in abstract thinking, which allows them to imagine the benefits of new practices more easily than people who need to see something right in front of them. Consequently, early adopters tend to make judgments on the merits of a proposed change earlier than the majority in a social group, mostly on the basis of their own personal assessments. Rogers found that many early adopters are considered opinion leaders by others in the same social group. Therefore, early adopters become the first real diffusers of an innovation—proactively and indirectly—by being the social group's early role models.

The early adopters, in turn, influence the next group—the *early majority*—those who respect the experience, insights, and evaluations of the opinion leaders. Rogers estimates that the early majority makes up roughly one-third of a social group. My hunch is that a good proportion of the early majority (as well as the innovators and early adopters) have a promotion-focused orientation—a concept we explored in chapter 2. Promotion-focused people look for new advantages and are motivated by what they can gain through change. As such, promotion-focused people may be among the first to adopt a change. The early majority are not as quick to embrace change as early adopters because the early majority relies more on discussion before coming to their assessments and judgments. In other words, the early adopters act more independently and the early majority act more collegially when adopting change. This need for discussion among the early majority, however, also helps facilitate the most dramatic diffusion of a new idea through a group, because the dialogue people engage in to help them make their own decisions spreads an idea—and evaluations of that idea—most widely and most quickly through a social system. My teenaged sons were early adopters of Facebook. My wife and I adopted it much later—only after much discussion with my teenagers, our family members, and friends. Eventually, we adopted Facebook as a means of keeping abreast with the lives of our teenagers.

The next adopter group—the *late majority*—are thought by Rogers to make up about another third of a social group. People in this group differ from the early majority by being more skeptical. They need more time and evidence to be convinced of the merits of making a change. Prevention-focused people may form a significant number of the late majority, as they are not motivated so much to attain the benefits of change but to avoid any losses. When promotion-focused people appreciate the benefits change will bring to them, they easily embrace change. The situation for prevention-focused people can be different, however. Anticipated loss can make it hard for this group to agree to change, and it can take them some time to balance the benefits against the losses to the point that change is acceptable for them. But in the end, change will probably convey for them some degree of loss. This group can be supported through change if their sense of loss can be acknowledged, reduced, or mitigated against.

Overall, the late majority is more adverse to risk and thus more cautious generally about change. For people in this group, most of the uncertainty about an innovation must be removed before they feel secure enough to adopt change. There is also a tendency among many people initially to overestimate the impact of proposed change, but as this group comes to understand that the impact will be less significant than they first supposed, they become more willing to accept change, since their sense of loss has become smaller. Rogers's own father was typical of late majority people, as he was initially skeptical of hybrid corn. But after several seasons of comparing his crop to that of his neighbors, he too became convinced it would improve his crop yield. The late majority are not resistant to change; rather, they reserve judgment on the merits of change. They have a wait-and-see attitude.

In this book I will refer to the late majority as *late adopters*. Congregational change becomes more likely as the size of the early majority increases. Consequently, a major goal of leaders in any planned change effort is to meet the needs of the skeptics so that they will choose to join the early majority sooner and contribute to the overall effort. Despite the efforts of leaders, however, some skeptics will want to wait and see, so leaders will always have late adopters to consider and help.

The final category of people are more than just skeptical: they are resistant to change. Their point of reference is the past rather than the future. They remain content with their current practices and see no reason to adopt new ways, despite what may be mounting evidence to the contrary. Rogers called the people in this group *laggards*. Laggards form unfavorable attitudes toward the proposed change early on, and those attitudes are often never open to reevaluation. While they are resistant to change, Rogers's choice to call the people in this group laggards implies that change may still be a possibility for them in time.

The graph in figure 4.2 shows Rogers's classic curve that illustrates the changing rate of adoption over time in a successful adoption of an innovation. It also shows the average proportion of people in the different adopter categories.[10] The rate of adoption is slowest initially, when those embracing a new idea are only the innovators and early adopters. The rate increases dramatically when the early and late

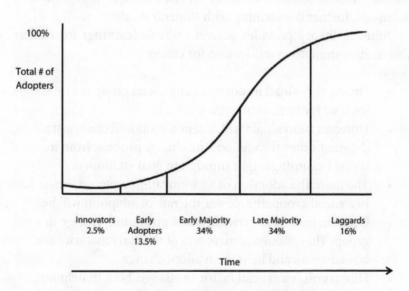

**Figure 4.2 Rate of Adoption of a New Idea by People in Different Adopter Categories**

majority begin to come on board with the innovation. The adoption rate again slows down, ultimately to zero, when only the resistant laggards remain. Compare this general representation of Rogers's theory to the graph for Facebook's adoption. Since 2008 the early and late majority have embraced this social medium and the adoption rate has been very high. Since April 1, 2011, however, a small but noticeable trend indicates that perhaps the adoption rate is now starting to slow down. The following table shows the net increase in total number of subscribers worldwide for each quarter since April 1, 2011.[11]

| June 30, 2011 | Sep. 30, 2011 | Dec. 31, 2011 | March 31, 2012 |
|---|---|---|---|
| 46,696,260 | 46,156,060 | 42,207,380 | 36,433,120 |

According to a *Wall Street Journal* article in June 2012, Facebook's user growth rate within the United States slowed sharply over the previous year.[12] It makes sense that Facebook's phenomenal growth is unsustainable, since not everyone has access to technology, some nations restrict access to Facebook, some people will never choose to use Facebook, and, ultimately, the number of humans is finite. It appears that the rate of adoption—in North America at least—is beginning to flatten out, further conforming with Rogers's model.

Diffusion theory provides several valuable learnings for leaders who wish to strengthen motivation for change:

- Only a very small minority in any social group are on the lookout for improvements.
- Different individuals will accept a proposed change at different times throughout the change process, from its initial beginnings right through to goal attainment.
- The more the adoption of an innovation relies on consensus in a social group, the slower the rate of adoption will be.
- Opinion leaders are critical when promoting change in a group. They influence members of the early majority and late adopters and help them adopt change.
- Discussion is a crucial factor in change, both in helping many people make their own decisions and in diffusing ideas, attitudes, and intentions.

- Some people are more motivated than others by the perceived benefits of change.
- People differ in their aversion to the risks of change.
- Some people will not be convinced on the theoretical merits of change, but will have to see concrete evidence of those merits with their own eyes during the implementation period.
- A group whose members appear to oppose a vision for a congregation's future is not a homogeneous group. Diffusion theory helps us appreciate that this group will be composed of the late adopters (who are the skeptics) and the laggards (who are the resistant). It is crucial for leaders to hold this distinction in mind because the two groups need to be dealt with differently. If leaders assume the opposition are all uniformly resistant to the vision, then leaders will run the risk of turning some skeptics (who are only late adopters) into the resistant (who may never accept the vision).
- Some people, despite being given every opportunity, argument, and evidence, will never change.

## Leading Motivation-Based Change

Both the transtheoretical model and diffusion theory explain how people experience change—individually and corporately. Motivational leaders seek to influence this experience so that the greatest number of people come to hold sufficient motives with sufficient priority that they will choose to change themselves. Four principles can be derived from the transtheoretical model and diffusion theory to help us create a step-by-step process that leaders can use to increase motivation for change.

First, organizations change as a consequence of the collective impact of individual change. Therefore, a process for leading change needs to emphasize individual change. Over the past fifteen years, a modest amount of work has been conducted to determine how the transtheoretical model may be applied to organizational change.[13]

Leaders start with the assumption that everyone begins in the precontemplation stage. The leaders' work, then, is to help all individuals in the organization shift into the contemplation stage and then into preparation, action, and maintenance, each stage in turn. Now, in smaller congregations, it is certainly possible for a leader to seek to influence each individual member, but this becomes more unrealistic in larger congregations. Regardless of congregational size, leaders need to work from the perspective that they are in the business of seeking to influence the attitudes, intentions, and actions of individuals.

The second principle we discover by combining these two theories is that it is not possible to ensure all the individuals of the organization will move through each stage of change simultaneously. As leaders help congregants move from contemplation through preparation, action, and maintenance, some people (such as the early adopters) will be ready to proceed to the next stage faster than others in the congregation (such as late adopters). Consequently, as leaders move into each new stage, they will need to work simultaneously with those who are ready to proceed, while continuing to work on the earlier steps with those who are not. In time, as the change process continues, leaders can conceivably be working with congregants who are dispersed

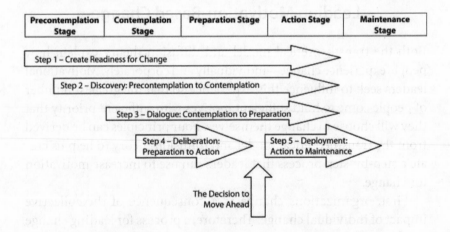

**Figure 4.3 The Transtheoretical Model's Alignment with the Motivation-Based Change Process**

throughout the different stages, trying to help individuals move from their current stage to the next.

The third principle we can derive from these theories is a consequence of the second. As leaders help individuals move through these stages, people will develop intentions and commitments to adopt and pursue a proposed goal at different times. In other words, there will be early adopters, an early majority, late adopters, and laggards. In congregational change,

- innovators should become leaders, since they are by definition the people who make changes to the established order of things. As leadership writer Max DePree writes, there is "one forgotten but essential truth about leadership: *Leaders have ideas.*"[14] Innovators are the first to realize while the congregation is in precontemplation that there are changes the congregation needs to make. In an ideal situation, the innovators would be the congregation's formal leadership (since innovation is the leaders' role), but this is not always the case.
- early adopters will emerge in the contemplation stage. They will understand the congregation's situation quickly and either think of their own solutions or adopt the proposed goals of the leaders.
- the early majority will emerge in the contemplation and preparation stages as a result of the influence of the leaders and the early adopters (who become opinion leaders). The early majority are also influenced by the discussions they conduct among themselves and with the late adopter members concerning the change initiative.
- late adopters will emerge near the end of the preparation stage of the process and during the action stage, due to their more cautious and skeptical nature. They are "late" because they begin to share the majority's intentions and commitments at the time the formal decision to proceed is made, and also after that point.
- the resistant (whom Rogers calls the laggards) can emerge at any time. While all those in the other adopter categories

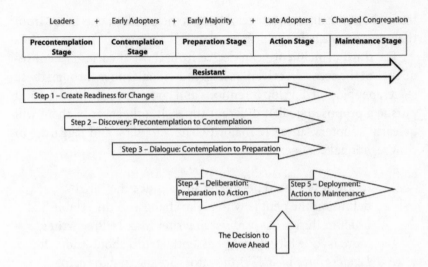

**Figure 4.4 Alignment of the Transtheoretical Model and the Adopter Categories of Diffusion Theory with the Motivation-Based Change Process**

by definition eventually develop the motivation to pursue a proposed goal, the resistant are unique in that they most likely will not.

Aligning Rogers's adopter categories with the stages of change of the transtheoretical model in this rigid way would not have been acceptable to Rogers himself. As a simple scheme, however, this alignment helps us anticipate the needs and roles of the different adopter groups as an organization's leaders pursue change. Figure 4.4 illustrates the scheme.

Think of a very long train crossing over a river on a bridge: it takes a while for the caboose to reach the other side of the river, where the engine is already traveling. Thinking of this analogy, the bridge is the point in the change process when people find themselves motivated to join others in agreeing to pursue a goal. The innovators and early adopters form the front part of the train—the engine, if you will. They are followed by the early majority and finally the late adopters. As for the resistant, they may join the train if the leadership makes the effort to help them do so.

A fourth principle derived from these two theories is that any process for change must be rooted in discussion. Discussion takes many forms, some that are very constructive and some that often are not. Dialogue facilitates increased mutual understanding in a group and can even enhance individuals' self-understanding as a consequence. Ultimately, dialogue can lead to changes in attitudes. Deliberation is a different form of discussion, focused on weighing the merits of an idea or direction. Deliberation can lead to choice making. Both forms of discussion are helpful in different stages of change, as we will see later in the chapter.

According to diffusion theory, early adopters as opinion leaders influence others' attitudes, especially those of the early majority, through discussion. Discussion also plays an important role in diffusing ideas, opinions, and attitudes throughout the social system via the early majority and late adopters. We will also see in the second half of the book that discussion is the leaders' best tool for discovering the initial attitudes and motives of congregants, and that, in turn, it can help leaders create a compelling vision for the future and a truly motivating change message. Finally, discussion ensures congregants are treated as a group of individuals rather than as a herd. Promoting discussion from precontemplation through contemplation, preparation, and action encourages everyone to reconsider their attitudes, intentions, and commitments. Discussion can be a forum for a growing understanding of current reality and for clarifying goals. It can also be the forum for people to affirm and strengthen each other's capability and context beliefs.

The *adaptive work* concept of Harvard's Ronald Heifetz reinforces this emphasis on discussion. Heifetz notes that during times of distress and change, people naturally look to leaders for assurance and help. But people can inappropriately expect their leaders to solve the riddles and make things better for them, when such solutions are not available as simple extensions of the congregation's current culture. Adaptive work is required when the problem is definable but no clear-cut solution is available. It is also required when a diversity of opinion about solutions exists. It is needed especially when the definition of the problem itself is not clear-cut. Heifetz says the critical diagnostic question is, "Does making progress on this issue require changes in people's values, attitudes or habits of behavior?"[15] If the answer is yes, then adaptive work is required, and the responsibility for addressing the issues must be shared broadly by the congregation. Only widespread discernment and discussion will help bring about the needed changes in people's motives, attitudes, intentions, and behaviors as well as develop the consensus necessary to enable change.

# A Process for Motivation-Based Change

Integrating the transtheoretical model with diffusion theory provides a framework for leaders to understand where, when, and how to intervene in the experience of change in order to strengthen people's motivation for change. The five steps of the motivation-based change process, introduced and discussed in this section, integrate not only these two theories but also the theology and psychology of motivation explained in chapters 2 and 3, as well as the online chapter.

## Step 1: Create Greater Readiness for Change

In every congregation at any particular time, some congregants are more ready for change than others. Having readiness for change means being receptive to new directions and having the ability to embark on a new path with ease. A greater readiness for change comes from a congregation's strong sense of stewardship of its own future and a consciousness of its hopes as well as its guiding values and priorities. Readiness for change can come from having a growth and improvement orientation. It can come from strong capability and context beliefs. Finally, readiness comes from having a congregational organization that can enable change effectively and highly trusted leaders to lead that change. The work of building readiness for change happens in the precontemplation stage because generally this work is done before a new initiative is considered.

Leading specific change is easier when congregants have a general readiness for change. Congregations with high readiness have a greater capacity to observe, analyze, and understand their current reality. They are also better able to understand proposed new initiatives and appreciate the reasons for those proposals. Experience has fostered strong general capability and context beliefs that are ready to be applied to a new challenge. Strong capability and context beliefs, in turn, help these congregations accept greater levels of risk and stress, which are so often inherent in change. These congregations already live at the transition boundary between precontemplation and contemplation. In summary, a congregation with a high readiness for change has a culture that embraces and pursues new aspirations with confidence. Given these many benefits, strengthening readiness for change should be the perpetual work of congregational leaders.

In an optimal situation, leaders first work at strengthening congregational readiness before a new initiative is even proposed. Leaders can also work at strengthening readiness during an actual change initiative, from precontemplation right through the action stage. This work is helpful, because individuals in an organization do not all proceed through change simultaneously; there will always be early and late adopters. Another reason to strengthen readiness continuously through a change initiative is that congregants proceeding through the steps from precontemplation through action gradually shift their thinking. In the contemplation stage, congregants have vague impressions regarding the need for change. By the time congregants enter the action stage, however, they are pursuing a sharply articulated goal. The work of creating readiness for change, then, shifts over time from a general readiness to pursue some kind of change to having a readiness to pursue a specific change.

How to strengthen readiness for change in a congregation is the focus of chapter 5.

## Step 2: Discovery

The discovery step fosters the initial shift people make from the precontemplation stage to the contemplation stage. The two goals of discovery are

- to help congregants begin to perceive a discrepancy gap between how things are and how they might be, and
- to help congregants begin to question their current attitudes and begin to formulate new attitudes.

The first goal fosters the sense that change is needed, while the second goal begins to create the motivation for change.

Individuals move out of precontemplation into the contemplation stage when attitudes shift from the belief that "things are fine" to dissatisfaction—a sense that something is not as good as it could be. But as we have seen, the sense of reality, perspective, frame of reference, or worldview of people in precontemplation may not be attuned enough to hear, understand, and appreciate proposals for change, often because new proposals come from perspectives, frames of reference, or worldviews different from their own. So to help congregants recognize a discrepancy, they need to be able to appreciate the discrepancy from the perspective of their current sense of reality, frame of reference, or worldview. Any discrepancy gap between how things are now and how things could be can create a sense of dissatisfaction, which can motivate people toward the contemplation stage. Early adopters begin to come into existence in this step because they are the first to really understand the discrepancy, they come to have a sense of urgency to do something about the discrepancy, and they even begin to see solutions for the gap.

The shift from precontemplation to contemplation is the best opportunity for leaders to influence the current attitudes of congregants and to encourage changed attitudes. Leaders will be ready to move on to the next step when most congregants

- appreciate that a discrepancy gap is real,
- start to imagine solutions to reduce the gap (which will eventually be defined in a goal or vision), and
- become aware of their current attitudes and begin to consider other attitudes.

Since people move through the stages of change at their own pace, some congregants will still be in precontemplation when the majority of the congregation shifts into the contemplation stage. This is to be expected and is the reason why leaders will need to continue to work at discovery while moving on to dialogue with the majority of congregants.

The discovery step—helping people shift from precontemplation to contemplation—is the focus of chapter 6.

## Step 3: Dialogue

The dialogue step helps congregants move from the contemplation stage to the preparation stage. The first goal of dialogue is to encourage the majority of individuals in the congregation to hold an intention to change. This happens through the continuing work of helping congregants develop new and stronger attitudes and evaluating the decisional balance among these attitudes so that the balance favors change. The second goal of this step is to formulate a goal or vision for the future that will satisfy congregants' motives that favor change. This goal or vision becomes the object of people's intentions.

Dialogue is not just a method to improve communications and solve problems. It is a deeper form of thoughtful discussion that seeks to discover shared meaning. In dialogue people come to a deeper appreciation of others and themselves, and of the beliefs and values that sustain a group's current culture and present attitudes. Through dialogue people can begin to share a new sensibility, learn how to think together, and discover new shared meaning together.

Developing a vision or goal for the future through dialogue improves motivation in two ways. First, dialogue about potential goals helps to surface the many motives of people for and against these goals as well as congregants' general attitudes that may or may not support these goals. Dialogue provides the opportunity for leaders to learn what goal is most motivating and why. In the long run, the most motivating goal (as compared to the most *logical* goal or the most *effective* goal) often has the greatest chance of being attained because it is the goal congregants can most easily get behind and pursue.

The second advantage of developing a vision or goal through dialogue is that it helps leaders create the change message. The change message is the articulation of the goal itself and the reasons (that is, motives) that the goal should be pursued. In the dialogue step, leaders learn the salient motives congregants hold that favor the goal, which the change message needs to highlight. Also during dialogue, leaders learn the motives that disfavor the goal, which need to be acknowledged and responded to in the change message. The learning about motives that takes place in dialogue provides the best preparation for leaders in the deliberation step.

Developing the future goal or vision creates both early adopters and many of the early majority, who recognize the need for change and see in this goal a way to reduce the discrepancy gap. At this point congregational leaders encourage early adopters to become opinion leaders, who are needed to widen discussions and influence direction, leading to an increase in the size of the early majority. But as the early majority forms, so too will the late adopters and the resistant, although at this point it may not be possible to distinguish between these two groups.

Discussing the concerns of the resistant during this step is prudent. When leaders give the resistant opportunity to shift from being critics to becoming collaborators, leaders provide the best conditions to help reduce both the number of the resistant and the power of their concerns. Also, by addressing the concerns of the resistant, leaders provide some of the greatest influence on late adopters. Late adopters are skeptics who require more reasons and evidence before they will accept change. The resistant can strongly influence late adopters because the resistant are visible critics of a proposed goal or vision whose arguments provide reasons and evidence for not pursuing the goal or vision. By dealing with the issues of the resistant, leaders help shift the decisional balance of late adopters toward their adoption of the goal or vision.

The discovery step helps congregants, through their current perspective, see an important discrepancy gap between how things are and how they might be. They come to appreciate *what* is happening. The dialogue step supports individuals as they analyze the *what* to learn *why* it is happening and begin to glimpse *how* to best respond to the discrepancy. Leaders can use this analysis to help congregants develop a new sense of their reality, perspective, frame of reference, or worldview. An improved perspective, in turn, allows congregants to become better analysts of their current reality and better out-of-the-box thinkers for imagining new directions. Consequently, congregants will begin to feel the *push* of concerns, which are arising from their new appreciation of current reality, and the *pull* of their hopes, which are articulated in emerging visions and goals for the future. When the drivers (the pros, the motives for change) outweigh the resisters (the cons, the motives against change), intentions to act are created. When these intentions surface for an emerging goal or vision for the future, leaders are ready to move into the next step.

The dialogue step is dealt with in chapter 7, and engaging the resistant is explored in chapter 9.

## Step 4: Deliberation

The deliberation step helps congregants move from the preparation stage to the action stage. The purpose of this step is to encourage as many congregants as possible to commit to the goal through their choice to act on their intentions. With goal commitment, congregants have the maximum motivation to pursue goal attainment. This is the persuasion phase during which the change message is developed and shared. During this step plans for goal attainment are developed. The change message and the plans strengthen the capability and context beliefs that are crucial for congregants to move from goal intention to goal commitment. This step ends with the formal decision to pursue the goal, that is, to enter the action stage.

The word *deliberation* is used to describe this stage because it reflects the changed nature of discussion in this step. Deliberation is a thoughtful discussion on a topic. It is the word we use when juries remove themselves from the courtroom to consider the evidence of a case. Deliberation leads to a choice regarding a matter before a group of people. During the deliberation step, congregants use this form of discussion to weigh the motives for and against the proposed goal. The work of all the previous steps combined with the change message create the context for the greatest number of people to enthusiastically say "Yes!" to the new initiative.

During deliberation, the rest of the early majority emerge, because their capability and context beliefs are strengthened by the change message and by what they see as logical, effective, and doable plans. The change message must provide clear and positive answers to the questions, Is there a way to do this? and, Are we able to do this? In this step leaders can also begin to see the late adopters and the resistant becoming more distinct. The congregational decision to pursue the vision through a proposed plan will bring the first late adopters on board with goal commitment. Seeing a majority of the congregation affirm the proposal is enough to answer the skepticism of some late adopters.

Leaders may still have some influence on the resistant during deliberation, but the likelihood of enrolling the resistant at this point is less than during the dialogue. During dialogue the sense of direction is still vague and flexible and thus possibly more adaptable to the concerns of the resistant. During deliberation the vision is more defined and less malleable, so it becomes harder to accommodate the interests of the resistant. But deliberation is the step that develops and communicates the change message. Persuasion—not accommodation—becomes the primary means leaders have to help the resistant join the majority at this point. Pastoral care of the resistant now becomes an emerging priority and will remain important through plan implementation as well as after the goal is attained.

The deliberation step is dealt with in chapter 8.

## Step 5: Deployment

The deployment step implements the plan to attain the vision or goal. It takes the congregation from preparation through the action stage to maintenance. There are four motivational concerns during this step. The first is to maintain the motivation of the congregation as it engages in the challenging and at times demoralizing implementation period. By reiterating the change message congregants can recall and reaffirm their motives for pursuing the goal. Using the train analogy again, it helps congregants remember the importance of the destination. High quality feedback also maintains motivation during deployment, because it helps congregants stay on track and moving toward the destination.

The second motivational concern of this step is for the late adopters. The deliberation step ends with the formal decision to proceed, at which time some late adopters will commit to the goal. Other late adopters will not, remaining skeptical during implementation and even until goal attainment. Leaders assist late adopters during this step by providing the evidence the skeptics need to help them choose goal commitment themselves.

The third motivational concern is for the resistant, who are tended to through the leaders' ongoing work of persuasion and pastoral care.

The final motivation concern of the deployment step comes at the end of the action stage. Achieving an envisioned future is a wonderful thing for a congregation to celebrate. From the perspective of motivating change, this celebration is also an excellent time to prepare the congregation for its next challenge, whatever and whenever that may be. Capability and context beliefs are attitudes developed by people's evaluations of their experience. The celebration of goal attainment should be a time to strengthen these two beliefs. By helping congregants appreciate that they are able to accomplish what they set their minds to and that their context is not a barrier to attaining their goals, congregants will have greater confidence to pursue new and greater goals in the future.

The deployment step is dealt with in chapter 10.

## Moving on to Application

This overview of the motivation-based change process wraps up our consideration of theory. The emphasis in the second half of this book will be the practical application of the theory as leaders work through the steps of the process. This process can be used just as it is all on its own. The motivation-based change process can also be used in tandem with other processes for planned change, of which there are many. You may have one you prefer. If you use a different process to lead change, the theory and practical suggestions of this book can provide an excellent supplement and support to ensure that you consider issues of motivation at the appropriate moments in the change process.

This description of the motivation-based change process is an idealized scheme, presented this way for ease of understanding. In reality, congregational change is messy, and at times the leaders' role in the midst of change can seem ambiguous at best. The congregation can get stalled in one stage of the transtheoretical model (which will tax the patience of leaders) and then perhaps rush unexpectedly through another stage (causing leaders to wonder if congregants have really completed the requisite work of the step). Thus, this process is intended as a guide rather than a prescription.

For example, this process directs leaders to focus on capability and context beliefs during the deliberation step because people need to develop confidence regarding their ability to attain the goal. People will frequently begin to express weak capability and context beliefs, however, in reaction to the discovery step because the emerging discrepancy gap challenges these beliefs. So while dealing with these beliefs is critical to the deliberation step, leaders may also find it important to encourage stronger capability and context beliefs earlier on in the process. If leaders don't, then congregants may fail to embrace a new initiative before they have even heard of it. As I frequently say in workshops, a process designed to fit all situations generally will generally fail to fit any one situation specifically. So again, use this process as a guide more than a rule.

Let us turn now to the practical use of this process.

# PART 2

# THE PRACTICE OF MOTIVATIONAL LEADERSHIP

## CHAPTER 5

# Preparing the Congregation: The Readiness for Change Step

*Available evidence shows that most public and private organizations can be significantly improved, at an acceptable cost, but that we often make terrible mistakes when we try because history has simply not prepared us for transformational challenges.[1]*
—John Kotter

Strengthening readiness for change is like plowing before planting: it prepares the ground to receive well the seed of a new idea. Readiness is a congregational attitude that allows a greater openness to change and enables a greater capacity to hear and appreciate new initiatives. By fostering a readiness attitude, leaders create the best possible context for the most people to make the greatest commitment to a new direction.

The concept of readiness for change is relatively new. The first landmark academic article on this topic was written only in 1993,[2] even though the concept was first proposed in 1957. Over the past twenty years, organization psychologists have found that a significant cause for resistance to change is an organization's lack of readiness. Consequently, creating readiness for change is now seen as a vital initial step on the path of motivating change.

Here is how one group of researchers amplified Kurt Lewin's classic formula for change in order to incorporate the key importance of readiness for change:

Successful implementation of organizational changes generally proceeds through three stages: readiness, adoption, and institutionalization. *Readiness* occurs when the environment, structure, and organizational members' attitudes are such that members are receptive to a forthcoming change. *Adoption* occurs when the organizational members temporarily alter their attitudes and behaviors to conform to the expectations of the change. *Institutionalization* occurs when the change becomes a stable part of members' behavior.[3]

Many congregational leaders operate on the premise that a change process begins when the leaders advocate the adoption of something new in congregational life, but (to continue the analogy) beginning the process at this point may be like throwing seed on rocky ground (where the idea establishes no roots) or among weeds (where the idea is choked to death by those around it). Creating good soil by building readiness for change helps congregants develop a clearer sense of the congregation's environment, an organizational structure for the congregation that facilitates change more readily, and foundational attitudes that improve the reception of any new idea. What follows are seven strategies for encouraging readiness for change.

## Strategy 1:
## Strengthen Congregational
## Stewardship of the Future

Readiness for change is enhanced by strengthening a congregation's stewardship of its future. According to organization psychologist Morela Hernandez at the University of Washington, strengthening stewardship values in an organization begins with leaders who understand themselves as stewards:

Leaders establish a positive cycle [of commitment to the future] by exhibiting stewardship behaviors that are in service of ensuring the wellbeing of future generations. Being a steward implies that the ultimate purpose of one's work is others and not self, that leaders do what they do for something larger than themselves, that their life's work may be the ability to lead but the final goal of this talent is other directed. These leaders demonstrate a responsibility to future generations to place the long-term best interests of others ahead of their self-interests. In doing so, they instill stewardship in their followers, an effect that is likely to be reciprocated as these followers become the future generation of leaders.[4]

This stewardship thinking has become a critical concern for a handful of organization psychologists, driven by their perception that the value of stewardship needs to be given greater priority in society. Our society's habits of accepting deficit budgets by governments, delaying responses to environmental concerns, preferring short-term profitability over long-term viability in our corporations, and supporting politicians who focus on their next election rather than the long-term well-being of their constituents are only a few examples of how we borrow from our children. "Intergenerational discounting" happens when the present generation chooses to benefit itself at the expense of future generations. Duke psychologist Kimberly Wade-Benzoni says we do this because of human nature:

> There is consensus among theorists and a convergence of empirical evidence that fairness judgments are typically biased in a self-serving manner, even though such subjective perceptions can appear objective and unbiased to moral reasoners themselves. . . . [In this way] individuals can have what they want and believe their actions to be fair.[5]

Our preference is not to incur costs to ourselves today for the sake of unknown people at some undetermined point in the future who, in the end, may not reap (or even need) the anticipated benefit we are asked to provide for them. Intergenerational discounting frequently happens in congregations as the answer to questions such as these:

- Do we spend our money today or establish a trust fund for tomorrow?
- Do we adopt new worship styles to appeal to the next generation of members or continue with a traditional style with which we are currently content?

- Do we defer maintenance on our historic building or repair it now for the sake of those who follow us?

People's sphere of concern for their congregation may not reach too far beyond the present, let alone for the generation of congregants that follows them. Psychologists are responding to this aspect of human nature by determining how to strengthen organizational stewardship so that people will give greater attention to future generations.

Wade-Benzoni in her extensive research has found that people tend to give greater consideration to future generations when they appreciate how past generations have served the present generation. When a congregation can look back at its history and see the decisions, contributions, and sacrifices of past generations that made a real difference for today's congregation, they in turn find themselves more inspired to do the same for the sake of the next generation. Fifty years ago, the congregation I serve was declining in a dying downtown neighborhood. They made the difficult decision to relocate to the southern edge of their city, even though that meant losing one-third of their members who chose to no longer be a part of the relocated congregation. But that decision, at that cost, was the principal reason our church grew to become one of the largest in our denomination. This story continues to inspire our congregation as it thinks about what we can do today for the sake of the congregation tomorrow. Our congregation today would like to leave the same kind of legacy. A negative role model can be just as inspiring. A congregation's past negligent maintenance of its heritage building (which has become a burden on the present congregation) can prompt the congregation to vow not to let the same thing happen to the congregation that follows them. Either way, the more a congregation appreciates that the benefit (or burden) experienced today is the result of the congregation's past stewardship (for better or worse), the more inclined it will be to demonstrate good stewardship of its future.

After all, today's congregation cannot pay back those who are now gone. Paying it forward becomes, in Wade-Benzoni's terms, intergenerational reciprocity. It applies "the golden rule over time," so that the others you "do unto" are those who come after you.[6] Intergenerational reciprocity is strengthened through the congregation's story. We frequently tell the story of our congregation's decision fifty years ago to move from downtown to the suburbs. In this way, congregants can learn that the stewardship of the future has always been important for St. Andrew's, that we benefit today because of it, and that we can do the same for those who follow us.

A congregation's stewardship of the future can also be strengthened when the congregation sees its future realities more clearly. The future, by its nature, always has an innate fuzziness.[7] Congregational commitment to the future increases with a greater sense of affinity with the congregation of the future, a more certain picture of what its future needs will actually be, and (if possible) a more specific time when the future congregation might benefit from actions taken in the present for the future's sake. The more real the future congregation becomes for congregants today, the more inclined today's congregation will be to help tomorrow's congregation.

Finally, people are motivated to act when they are confident that what they do today will have enduring value. For example, Wade-Benzoni has found that "a number of scholars have linked the desire for symbolic immortality to concern and commitment to future generations as expressed through activities aimed at leaving a positive legacy of the self for the future."[8] Helping people deepen their sense of stewardship of the future in this way—by assuring them that they are leaving a legacy—appeals to their sense of moral identity ("Being generous for the sake of the next generation expresses who I am") and their sense of having enduring influence in the world. Both motives have been found to be particularly important when there is a time lag between present action and future benefit.

Notice that strengthening a congregation's stewardship of its future is not about setting goals and making plans. It is about building an attitude of gratitude for the past (which provides people with a model for present action) and a deeper sense of solidarity with the future congregation (which provides a greater sense of responsibility in present action). These, in turn, provide motivational energy to concerns felt today, strengthening commitment to do something for the sake of tomorrow.

# Strategy 2:
# Strengthen Capability and Context Beliefs

Before congregants will commit to pursue any goal, they need positive answers to two questions: Are we capable of attaining this goal? Will our context allow us to attain this goal? The answers will depend on how a congregation interprets its past experience of pursuing endeavors and meeting challenges. The best way to engage people's capability and context beliefs is to help people recall congregational stories of past challenges and successes. Recalling these stories with satisfaction and pride creates the observation "Yes, we did!" and a confidence about future endeavors—"Yes, we can!" Such stories provide the evidence people need to trust in their own abilities when striving for goals and to trust in their capacity to deal with their context. Readiness for change is strengthened when a congregation holds these two kinds of trust.

Stories of congregational success may not be evident to the leadership at first, but this does not mean that such stories do not exist for your faith community. The story of every congregation is multifaceted, intricate, and convoluted, so congregants make their story understandable through the use of interpretive themes and narrative scripts. The themes and scripts habitually used may not carry the congregation's sense of capability and context beliefs, so leaders may need to help congregants learn and remember their stories of the congregation through themes and scripts that do convey these beliefs.

For example, our congregation is currently considering the creation of a new social ministry for families in the south of Calgary. The fact that "we've never done that before" could call our capability and context beliefs into question. The current dominant interpretive theme in our congregation's story reminds us that we are a missional church, but this does not mean a "ministry for families" can't also become an interpretive theme as well. In fact, the large majority of our mission involvements have always been with families in need, but we don't recognize this persistent focus because we don't tell our story in a way that highlights it. Retelling our story through a new, authentic narrative theme helps us understand that our passion in mission has always been dominated by concern for families. The fact that we have had significant success assisting families in need in many smaller ways will strengthen our capability and context beliefs as congregants are given the opportunity to hear these stories about the congregation in a different way.

Context beliefs can be strengthened by telling the congregation's story in a way that illustrates the minimal impact context had in past change efforts. I find that congregational stories about change tend to focus on the congregation itself and overlook the significance of the context. These self-centered stories can be amplified to include details about how the barriers to change anticipated in the wider community turned out not to exist, or how the people in the wider community were receptive and helpful to the congregation in surprising ways. Hearing their congregation's own story in these new ways can strengthen congregants' motivation to pursue new initiatives because it fosters congregants' internal locus of control beliefs.

If you don't think your congregation has enough positive stories about attaining goals, then create new stories. A congregation's capability and context beliefs can be strengthened through the pursuit of a few challenging but quite attainable goals during the precontemplation stage. Attaining a few goals in this way can foster a greater sense of mastery and strengthen capability and context beliefs, preparing the congregation for more significant challenges.

## Strategy 3:
## Change Perceptions of Current Reality

Most congregants will readily agree that big changes have taken place in their congregation's context in recent decades, but many congregants will not appreciate the significant impact of those changes on their own faith community, for both today and tomorrow. Developing a clear view of their congregation's current reality can help congregants move toward the precontemplation-contemplation border.

The most arresting example of this that I've experienced recently came from a 2008 study of religion in Canada conducted by sociologist Reginald Bibby. His survey revealed that 47 percent of Canadian teenagers had never attended a worship service of any kind for any religion.[9] The other 53 percent of Canadian teens included those who had attended even just one service. When I shared this statistic in a sermon one Sunday morning, you could hear eyes popping out of people's heads. This statistic simply and graphically demonstrates the difficulties Canadian congregations face today in being faithful and effective stewards of their future. A clear understanding of current reality can foster concern and a greater urgency to act.

## Strategy 4:
## Bank Trust Always

Readiness for change does not depend solely on a congregation's beliefs about itself. It also depends on a congregation's beliefs about its leaders. Trust is the currency of leadership, and the greater a congregation's trust in its leaders, the greater will be the congregation's readiness for change. Think of trust like money invested in the stock market: it can be slow to build up, lost quickly, and if lost, so very hard to recoup. Proposed change typically elicits some degree of anxiety, because change asks people to go where they've never been before. Trust, however, strengthens hope and reduces anxiety.

Trust can be hard to come by in our insecure and skeptical culture, so leaders need to be mindful of building and maintaining the trust people have in them. Trust is strengthened when leaders exhibit the three qualities that inspire trustworthiness: benevolence (our leaders have our best interests at heart), ability (our leaders can do what they promise to do), and integrity (our leaders will do what they promise to do).[10] Trust is also rooted in the leaders' reputation for good judgment, wisdom, and prudence. Trust is built when leaders are seen and known to take to heart the interests of people by showing concern, respect, and fairness. Good communications strengthen trust, a matter I will discuss further in chapters 7 and 8. And when a mistake is made, putting banked trust at risk, an honest and sincere acknowledgment, an apology, and changed ways go a long way to regaining some trust. Confession is good not only for the soul.

An example: The leaders of one congregation in Ontario recognized that it was time to consider adding to and renovating the church facilities. A building committee was created; it was composed of congregational members who were experts in the congregation's life, building design, and construction. It included the senior pastor. This group worked in isolation for about a year to develop a practical and financially realistic proposal for facility expansion that would truly meet the congregation's needs. When the schematic diagrams of the new facility were revealed, the congregation asked with one voice, "Where did this come from?" Even though the plan was virtually perfect in every way, the congregation overwhelmingly rejected the proposal, substantially because they had not been involved in the process. Trust in the congregation's leaders declined significantly, with lasting fallout. This building committee licked its wounds and began planning anew through an extremely open, participatory process, but the congregation ignored it. There was a high level of skepticism among people as they wondered whether the new open process was simply window dressing. In the end, renewing the planning process entailed laying the project aside for a few years, changing the people on the committee, naming a new convener, and the departure of their pastor. In the meantime, however, the delay meant that the recognized facility needs of the congregation remained unmet for six years.

Trust, which can take significant time to build, can be lost so very quickly and hard to recoup. If you are conscious of maintaining and strengthening trust, you are building readiness for change.

## Strategy 5:
## Organize for Greater Readiness

What do members of the governing board of your congregation believe about their role? Do they think of themselves as leaders or managers? Are they permission withholding or permission granting? Do they want to spend their time reflecting on the big picture or micromanaging the organization? How the governing board views their work can have a big impact on the congregation's readiness for change.

Our congregation, like many, has a committee structure. We Presbyterians like to think of the role of the governing board (the session) as providing oversight, which means supervising what committees do. When I arrived at St. Andrew's, the practice of our session was primarily to reconsider, rework, and redirect what had already been decided and done by committees. This approach to governance not only disempowers and frustrates the members of those committees but it also leads to long board meetings focused on minutiae. Consequently, little time remained for doing the work of leadership: reflecting on the callings of Christ to the church, assessing the effectiveness of our organization, discovering emerging needs and concerns, and plotting new directions for congregational life. Over a period of two years or so, I helped the session come to hold new beliefs about itself: that the session was primarily a leadership body that can empower and trust the committees to fulfill their responsibilities. In time, the session became content to receive one- or two-paragraph reports from each committee. Eventually, the only recommendations the session wanted to receive from committees were for either major initiatives or changes in a committee's mandate. The time given to oversight was reduced to forty to sixty minutes, which freed up a significant block of time for the session to apply itself to its leadership role.

This story illustrates one way the organization of a congregation can be reshaped to create greater readiness for change, since the governing board needs the time and perspective to consider change. But organizing for greater readiness can take other forms as well:

- The congregation might need an executive group or a long-range planning team to support the board's work.
- The implementation of any new idea will take people's time and energy. If the current organization already takes people's available time and energy, then it may need to be restructured in order to free up people so that effort can be given to new initiatives.
- New projects could be assigned to new task groups, composed of people interested in the issue and who have leadership skills. Standing committees of a congregation often have full agendas and approach their work with management (rather than leadership) mindsets. It can be ineffective (and inconsiderate) to assign new projects

to committees that already have a full and important
workload.

Increased organizational effectiveness creates a capacity to consider
and effect change, so improving organizational effectiveness fosters
greater readiness for change.

## Strategy 6:
## Choose and Train Leaders for Greater Readiness

Readiness for change can be improved by inviting the congregation's
best leaders to take formal leadership roles in the congregation. In addition to the usual qualities one looks for in leaders, good candidates

- have positive attitudes toward the congregation and a
  commitment to it;
- will likely be in the contemplation stage while the large
  majority of congregants are in precontemplation, since good
  leaders are always scanning for discrepancy gaps;
- exhibit a stewardship of the future;
- have a promotion focus that motivates them to pursue
  improvements in congregational life;
- are innovators who are comfortable with promoting
  changes to the established order of things;
- have generally good capability and context beliefs, which in
  turn foster a leader's self-confidence;
- are already opinion leaders in the congregation; and
- exhibit the three qualities that inspire trustworthiness:
  benevolence, ability, and integrity.

Congregational governing bodies are not always populated with such
people, and that can make congregational change very hard indeed.
Certainly, training the current leaders can and will improve their capacity to lead, so training is always a worthy pursuit. In fact, pursuing
the first five strategies in this chapter with congregational leaders will

enhance their capacity to lead. If a congregation's leaders do not have a readiness for change, then the congregation itself will never have it.

But in reality not everyone who is currently a leader may be gifted for it. Replacing these people with more gifted leaders, through a procedurally fair process, can result in the single greatest improvement in readiness for change.

## Strategy 7:
## Foster Readiness for Change by Evaluating It

The first six strategies address different aspects of congregational life to improve readiness for change. An important role of congregational leaders is to analyze the congregation's motivational climate to determine which strategies to apply. Through analysis leaders can determine the following:

- What characteristics of the congregation already reflect its readiness for change? How can the leaders build on them?
- What characteristics of the congregation illustrate its lack of readiness? Which of these can the leaders address and improve?

What follows is a general readiness-for-change audit that lists many of the most important readiness characteristics. The more statements you can affirm are true for your congregation, the more confident you can be that it is ready for change.

You can conduct this evaluation yourself for initial insights, but this tool can be even more helpful if your congregation's board completes it. Each person can complete this audit and then share his or her insights with the other board members. As the group works through the different statements, board members will unanimously affirm some as true or untrue for your church. These identify the aspects of your congregation's life that you know will promote or inhibit change. Rich discussion can happen when board members disagree over particular statements, which can lead to a deeper mutual understanding about your church.

## How Ready Are We to Think about Our Future?

This survey, the "Readiness for Change Questionnaire," asks you to assess our congregation's readiness to pursue new goals and directions. The following statements are all phrased positively.

Use a scale of 1 to 4, where:

1 = Very True for Us
2 = Somewhat True for Us
3 = Somewhat Untrue for Us
4 = Quite Untrue for Us

Circle the appropriate number. If you do not know, or if you think a statement is neither true nor untrue for us, please leave it blank. What we wish to know is which readiness conditions listed on the questionnaire will help or hinder our pursuit of new goals.

As you can see from this checklist, a great range of characteristics in the life of your congregation can strengthen and weaken readiness. Once your leadership group has made its assessment, invite them to consider how to build on the strengths and address the weaknesses. In fact, the "not true" statements can become an agenda for change in and of themselves. In addressing these different issues within your congregation, you will be not only building readiness for change but at the same time generally improving congregational life for the better. In the congregation I currently serve, we spent more than three years working on many of these characteristics. While that may seem like a long time, it is truly an investment that pays significant dividends, increasing the imagination, energy, excitement, and confidence that congregants will have when it comes to the dreaming and planning stage.

## Strengthening Specific Readiness for Change

As stated in chapter 4, leaders need to work at strengthening readiness for change throughout the motivation-based change process, since people get on board with a proposed initiative at different times

# Readiness for Change Questionnaire

| *Readiness Characteristic* | *Response* | | | |
|---|---|---|---|---|
| The congregation is generally open to change. | 1 | 2 | 3 | 4 |
| The congregation has a positive history of effectively implementing new ideas. | 1 | 2 | 3 | 4 |
| The congregation is able to take risks. | 1 | 2 | 3 | 4 |
| There are no old scars that may become open wounds if the congregation begins to consider its future. | 1 | 2 | 3 | 4 |
| The congregation has the core confidence it needs to do new things. | 1 | 2 | 3 | 4 |
| The congregation has the flexibility needed to bring new ideas to life. | 1 | 2 | 3 | 4 |
| The congregation is capable of living with the stress of making change. | 1 | 2 | 3 | 4 |
| The congregation is more mission-minded rather than focused on maintaining the status quo. | 1 | 2 | 3 | 4 |
| The congregation is inclined more toward serving others rather than serving itself. | 1 | 2 | 3 | 4 |
| The congregation focuses more on its future rather than on today or yesterday. | 1 | 2 | 3 | 4 |
| The congregation is strongly motivated by its faith to take on new initiatives. | 1 | 2 | 3 | 4 |
| The culture of the congregation permits and enables change. | 1 | 2 | 3 | 4 |
| The congregation is very aware of the changing nature of our society, and that awareness in turn helps shape the congregation's ministry and mission. | 1 | 2 | 3 | 4 |
| The congregation's current level of satisfaction, loyalty, commitment, and happiness will support change. | 1 | 2 | 3 | 4 |
| There are no pockets of negativity among the people of the congregation. | 1 | 2 | 3 | 4 |

| Readiness Characteristic | | Response | | |
|---|---|---|---|---|
| The congregation is able to have honest, thoughtful, and helpful discussions about new ideas and initiatives. | 1 | 2 | 3 | 4 |
| People who disagree are able to engage each other in open and healthy ways. | 1 | 2 | 3 | 4 |
| The congregation is free of distracting conflict. | 1 | 2 | 3 | 4 |
| When a decision is made, the congregation is able to rally behind it. | 1 | 2 | 3 | 4 |
| Those who are highly respected in our congregation are known to support new initiatives that have been formally approved by the congregation or its leaders. | 1 | 2 | 3 | 4 |
| There are no turf issues that could become a problem. | 1 | 2 | 3 | 4 |
| People in the congregation generally believe the congregation is managed well. | 1 | 2 | 3 | 4 |
| The congregation trusts its leaders. | 1 | 2 | 3 | 4 |
| Congregation leaders are prepared to consider the congregation's future and are able to commit to adopted goals. | 1 | 2 | 3 | 4 |
| The leaders are able to carry the stress of implementing congregational change. | 1 | 2 | 3 | 4 |
| The governance structures and rules will help us achieve new goals. | 1 | 2 | 3 | 4 |
| The congregation's habits for making decisions and implementing plans will help take a new initiative from goal to reality. | 1 | 2 | 3 | 4 |
| The congregation has adequate financial and human resources to engage in change. | 1 | 2 | 3 | 4 |
| The congregation believes that it can do whatever it sets its mind to. | 1 | 2 | 3 | 4 |
| The general mood of the congregation overall is positive. | 1 | 2 | 3 | 4 |

during the process. But there is a second reason for constantly working at building readiness: as the change process unfolds, people become clearer about what is changing and why. The clarity of purpose, goal, or vision in turn helps leaders to tailor their interventions using the first six strategies so that the strategies can have their greatest impact. In other words, clarity of purpose, goal, or vision makes it possible to foster greater readiness for a specific change.

Consider as an example strengthening of the congregation's stewardship of the future. We know that future stewardship is diminished by the future's innate fuzziness: the uncertainty regarding who the future congregation will be, what its real needs will be, and when those needs will need to be met. Some of this fuzziness is reduced when a congregation develops clear understanding regarding its current reality, because this understanding can be used to develop a reasonable and probable scenario of what the future congregation will look like if the status quo is allowed to continue. When a scenario like this is shared with the congregation, the scenario helps leaders say, "If we do not act today, then this will be the consequence for the next generation of our church." Generally, people do not like the feeling that their actions could have a negative impact on others, including unknown others in their future. Consequently, people may feel moved to mitigate this feeling by acting now for the sake of the future. On the positive side, a scenario like this strengthens intentions to leave a legacy, because people appreciate how current action may reduce the probability of the scenario becoming a future reality. A vivid and realistic scenario gives people a greater certainty that the need will be real and today's help will be appreciated.

Clarity of purpose, goal, or vision can also help leaders make their interventions through the other strategies more specific. For example, when a clear goal or vision for the future emerges later in the process, leaders are better positioned to strengthen congregational capability and context beliefs by addressing specific capabilities and relevant contexts. Having a specific goal also helps leaders arrange for a vicarious experience of mastery by finding congregations that have already pursued and attained the same goal and to derive from them stronger capability beliefs. Congregational stories can also be retold through the theme of the goal or vision, highlighting how the congregation in the past endeavored to meet similar challenges. With regard to leadership, goal clarification can provide the criteria for leader recruitment, because you want leaders who are best able to pursue the specified goal. Training leaders is also easier when goals are clear, because the goal makes clear what knowledge and skills will be needed for attainment. Goal clarity also helps reorganization of congregational structures to create the ways and means needed to attain the goal most effectively.

## Moving On to the Discovery Step

Discovery is the first step of a planned change process regarding a specific issue. There are no definite criteria to determine when to begin discovery. Choosing when to commence the motivation-based change process will depend on the leaders' assessment of the importance and urgency of the challenge before the congregation and congregants' readiness to address the challenge. But change is often thrust upon congregations at inopportune moments, leaving no time for leaders to strengthen readiness.

This chapter began with the analogy that strengthening readiness for change is like plowing before planting. As Paul reminded the Corinthian congregation, "You are God's field" (1 Cor. 3:9). In this passage Paul was referring to the growth in discipleship of the Corinthian Christians, also using a farming metaphor: "I planted, Apollos watered" (v. 6). Leaders are like farmers, since both bring growth and change. But if we are *God's* field, then building readiness and encouraging change is not our work alone. If we are God's field, then we are recipients of God's grace as well, which comes like rain and sunshine. Readiness can be strengthened by remembering who we are and receiving this grace. This is an encouraging reminder for leaders as they enter the discovery step and, like Paul, plant the seed of a new idea: God's grace was already with God's field before the plowing and planting. So, leaders need not fret over the exact, right time to plant.

## CHAPTER 6

# Encouraging Attitude Change:
# The Discovery Step

*You can't get there from here.*[1]
*—Ogden Nash*

In discovery, congregants begin to focus on change. Discovery helps congregants

- perceive a discrepancy gap between how things are and how things might be. A discrepancy gap describes what could be changed.
- reconsider—and hopefully change—current attitudes. Changed attitudes create motivation for change.

The work of leaders is to influence people so that they come to share enough common attitudes of sufficient strength that a group will develop a common intention to act.

## The Leader's Preliminary Work for Discovery

The urge to lead comes from an attitude formed by the leader. An issue in the congregation's life becomes an *attitude object*. The leader forms beliefs about the object that suggest something has to change. The belief is evaluated motivationally and prompts the leader's action. The attitude may be held strongly, which fosters strong intentions. But before acting, leaders should reflect on their own attitudes about the issue by asking questions such as these:

- *Is the issue I have in mind the real issue?* As a leader, you need to be very clear for yourself that the object of your attitude is really the most salient issue for the congregation.
- *What is the basis for my own beliefs about this issue?* Have those beliefs arisen from what you have learned, experienced, or figured out yourself? Are these beliefs adequate? Should you examine them more fully?
- *Why do I feel the urge to intervene as a leader on this issue?* What are your motives for acting on this issue?
- *Are my motives biased in some way?* In other words, are you being motivated by the most appropriate motives? For example, a desire to avoid conflict over an issue can bias the evaluation we make about our belief or downplay our motivation to act. Thinking about our personal motives and why they are important to us keeps us honest and ethical.
- *What other attitudes do I have toward this issue?* We can have several attitudes about a single issue that can lead us to evaluate the issue differently. Why does the decisional balance of your attitudes motivate you to act?

Once you have reflected on your own attitudes, you are better prepared to take a second preliminary step: to think about congregants' relevant attitudes toward the issue. Leaders need to take this step to prepare themselves for the real work of the discovery step. The questions used to reflect on congregational attitudes are much the same as the questions leaders pose to themselves:

- *How aware is the congregation of the issue that gives you concern?* In precontemplation, congregants may not be mindful of the issue giving you concern, although some may.

- *Will congregants see the real issue, or will they be convinced that the concern reflects a different issue?* This question helps you assess the educational work required to help congregants appreciate the situation.
- *What might congregants believe about this issue?* This question gets at the core of attitudes. What beliefs about the issue are most prevalent and most powerful? Have these beliefs arisen from what congregants have learned, experienced, or figured out on their own? Will these beliefs promote or inhibit change?
- *In forming their attitudes, how have congregants evaluated their beliefs?* This question starts to get at congregational motives for acting or not acting. Ask yourself why congregants might have evaluated their beliefs in these ways.
- *What other attitudes do congregants have toward this issue?* Congregational attitudes are never homogeneous, with some attitudes being more prevalent and motivating than others.

Conducting this kind of reflection among a group of leaders—rather than just on your own—generates deeper insight. The best insight, however, comes through inquiries made of the congregants themselves. Casually ask people about their thoughts on the issue and why they believe what they believe about the issue. You can also ask people what others (not naming names) might think about the issue. Through simple conversations you can learn more completely what the prevailing attitudes are, what beliefs are contained in those attitudes, and how strongly attitudes are held. Along the way, you may also discover the potential early adopters for new directions as well as those who might be resistant to change.

The next step is to weigh the relative importance of the various attitudes. In chapter 2, I described a helpful tool for doing this evaluation, called force field analysis. Leaders can use it to assess the motives dispersed throughout the congregation that will promote and resist change. This exercise is best conducted by your leadership group and unfolds as follows:

1. On sheets of newsprint, set up two columns entitled "Drivers" and "Resisters."
2. Drivers are motives that favor change, and resisters are motives that oppose change. List under the appropriate heading as many motives you can think of. Don't worry whether you are confusing beliefs, attitudes, or motives. Simply list them all.

| Drivers | Resisters |
|---------|-----------|
| • ---------------- | • ---------------- |
| • ---------------- | • ---------------- |
| • ---------------- | • ---------------- |
| • ---------------- | • ---------------- |
| • ---------------- | • ---------------- |
| • ---------------- | • ---------------- |
| • ---------------- | • ---------------- |
| • ---------------- | • ---------------- |
| • ---------------- | • ---------------- |

3. Rank the drivers and resisters for the strength of their influence: weak, medium, or strong.
4. For the drivers, consider (a) which ones will provide the greatest possible leverage for positive change (these are ones you want to capitalize on) and (b) which drivers can be strengthened in their importance. For the resisters, consider (a) which ones exert the greatest influence opposing change (these are the ones you want to give significant attention to) and (b) which resisters can be diminished in their importance. You will recall the teeter-totter illustration from chapter 2. The goal here is to figure out how to change the balance of influence so that the drivers become more influential compared to the resisters, tilting the balance toward acceptance and away from rejection of change.

When you have finished this assessment, you will have chosen the most important motives you will want to address. For now, we have jumbled motives and attitudes together as sort of the same thing. Later, as you seek to influence people's attitudes, you will need to break the attitudes down into their components—belief, evaluation, and strength—in order to encourage attitudinal change. If you can help people change either the belief, the evaluation, or the strength, then you have helped them change their attitude, and given the situation, changing one of these attitude components may be easier than changing either of the other two.

At this point, you have completed the necessary preparatory work:

- You are clear on the issue you wish the congregation to address (the attitude object).
- You are aware of your own attitudes toward the issue: your beliefs about the issue, where those beliefs came from, and why you consider them important. In other words, you are aware of your motives and why they motivate you.
- You have assessed the diversity of attitudes held by congregants, determining which ones will help and hinder change.

If the work of leadership is to influence people so that they come to share enough common attitudes of sufficient strength that a group will develop a common intention to act, then at this stage you know which motives you want to address. That is, you know which straws you want to draw out from the bales and which motives you want eased back into the bales of all those bales in the barn. Armed with this information, you are now ready to raise the issue for public discussion by helping people discover a discrepancy gap.

## Discovering a Discrepancy Gap

A twenty-one-year-old elder was invited to chair a new congregational committee for church growth—a pretty new idea in that day. The young man agreed readily because he thought church growth was an important goal for the congregation's future. The new committee members were all equally enthusiastic as they set to work learning about this new ministry focus. Over the months that followed, this group came to understand the perspectives, principles, and practices of church growth and slowly developed a growth strategy that would fit their congregation. After about five months' worth of work, the committee made its first presentation to the board. At the conclusion, the young elder asked for questions but heard only silence. Finally, one lonely question was asked, "Why would we be interested in church growth when we are one of the largest congregations in our denomination?" The continuing silence suggested that the same question was on everyone's mind. The proposals went nowhere, and within two months the church growth committee faded out of existence.

I was that twenty-one-year-old elder, and I was angry, disappointed, and disillusioned. Not until years later did I appreciate our committee's naiveté in presenting our proposals without first preparing the session for them. Most of the elders did not have the same concerns and priorities held by the committee members. The elders did not share the five-month journey of learning that benefitted the committee. The elders assumed that the current numeric strength of the congregation would simply continue as it always had. They had what is called *earned complacency*, which is the tacit belief that simply maintaining what proved successful in the past will create ongoing success. They did not appreciate, as the committee had come to learn, that the mounting impact of societal change on the congregation would lead to a significant decline in membership. Over the following twenty-five years, the congregation's membership declined by 69 percent and its church school enrollment declined by 87 percent.

Today I can't blame the board for its decision, since the church growth committee did nothing to help the elders change their thinking. To start with, the majority of elders had little readiness for change. But our committee also failed to show the leaders that the congregation's current reality was not as healthy as elders believed. Unless people can discover that an actual gap exists between how things are now and how things could be or should be, they will have little interest in change. Making people aware that a discrepancy gap exists is necessary if congregations are going to move from the precontemplation to the contemplation stage, because a discrepancy gap helps people become dissatisfied with the status quo. If change is like a rocket ship that takes people from the earth to the moon, then the discrepancy gap is the rocket's launching pad. Without the launching pad, "you can't get there from here." Leaders can help congregants discover a discrepancy gap in congregational life and grow in dissatisfaction about it through four different strategies.

## Strategy 1: Discover a Current Reality Gap

A current reality gap exists when congregants become aware, in some way, of their current reality. This approach asks the essential question, Is our view of our current reality actually current? Recall my story of the church growth committee. The elders responded to our proposals by saying that since our church was one of the largest in our denomination, there was no need to think about growth. A history of numeric strength fostered an attitude that numeric strength would continue. The committee could have helped the session immensely by asking, "Is that belief actually true?" We easily could have shown the leaders the significant numeric decline experienced by the congregation over the previous fifteen years: in membership from 1,749 to 1,398, in number of baptisms annually from 91 to 23, in church school enrollment from 730 to 169. The elders would all have been vaguely aware of these trends but not truly mindful of them. A current reality check like the one above describes *what* is happening, which then provides the opportunity to explore *why* it is happening. If our church growth committee had taken this approach, our board would probably have responded to our report with concern and listened to our recommendations with interest.

Many leaders will tailor their own approach to help their particular congregation assess its current reality. Diagnostic tools, such as SWOT analysis (through which people name their organization's strengths, weaknesses, opportunities, and threats), can be borrowed from the business world as well. Others prefer current reality diagnostic tools designed specifically for congregational use. Kennon Callahan's *Twelve Keys to an Effective Church* helps a congregation evaluate itself through "twelve factors [that] have emerged persistently as the central characteristics of successful missional churches."[2] Natural Church Development centers on a diagnostic tool that assesses the overall health of a congregation. Willow Creek's Spiritual Life Survey reveals the spiritual well-being of a congregation. These three use prescriptive analysis, which creates a discrepancy gap between the congregation's current reality and what the packaged program prescribes as the optimal conditions for a congregation. These diagnostic tools create current reality gaps, because the tools show people that their assumptions that "things are fine" are wrong, which in turn fosters concern. The tools help the gap become an attitude object for congregants and help people form beliefs about the attitude object and evaluate it negatively ("Our situation needs to be improved. We must act"). Current reality gaps elicit push motives for change.

These diagnostic tools have disappointed many leaders because their congregations did not act on the information revealed by the tools. But these programs are designed primarily to foster an appreciation that a discrepancy gap exists. While perceiving a discrepancy gap does foster some motivation to change, congregants often need more motivation than is created by a discrepancy gap alone. It is too easy for leaders to expect too much from such tools.

## Strategy 2: Discover an Ideal-Reality Gap

The second approach is to discover an ideal-reality discrepancy gap. This approach asks the essential question, How can we fulfill more fully one of the great callings of the church? With an ideal-reality gap, a calling of the church becomes an attitude object for congregants and helps people form stronger beliefs about the calling and to evaluate the attitude object positively, so that people desire to close the gap between reality and the ideal. Ideal-reality gaps elicit pull motives for change. Some congregational leaders prefer to identify the ideal over discovering a current reality gap, because they prefer what they perceive to be a more positive orientation of this strategy.

Our church growth committee could have introduced our report using the theme of the Great Commission to make disciples. We could have retold the story of how our congregation since 1844 had successfully handed on the Christian faith from generation to generation, fulfilling the Great Commission, and seen numeric growth as a consequence. We could then have presented how our generation was doing by comparison, speaking of the new challenges faced in our rapidly changing society. We could have asked the elders to evaluate our practices for introducing people to the Christian faith and strengthening people's discipleship, with the goal of enhancing what we do to become even more effective in fulfilling the Great Commission. Ideal-reality discrepancy gaps foster desire and anticipation, which arise from the pull motives of people's hopes.

An excellent process for facilitating this kind of discussion is called the World Café,[3] which is a consensus-building process based on small group dialogue. A room is set up like a café with scattered tables that can seat four or five people. Participants discuss "a question that matters" for twenty to thirty minutes. At the end of the first round of discussion, one person remains at the table as the host while the rest join people at other tables. These "travelers" carry the key ideas, themes, and issues from their first conversation to the next, now with a completely new group of travelers. The table host introduces the next round of discussion by briefly highlighting the conversation that happened at that table during the first round of dialogue. Dialogue is held again, with participants developing their thoughts through cross-pollination with the previous discussions. A third and even fourth round of discussion can be held. In the final round, participants return to their original table to compare notes, synthesize insights, and begin to see if a consensus is emerging. The exercise ends with the table hosts reporting on the ideas coming out of the last discussion.

It is quite common to hear a great deal of consensus arising from all the table groups at the end of the exercise. The success of this process depends on having a meaningful question to discuss. As the creators of this process say, "Well-crafted questions attract energy and focus our attention on what really counts. . . . They should invite inquiry and discovery vs. advocacy and advantage."[4] If we think again about the Great Commission as a calling, I can imagine conducting two separate rounds of the World Café using two different questions. The first round could discuss the question, Why is the Great Commission important to the church? The answers to this question are a congregation's motives to fulfill this calling. These motives in turn become the rationale for a congregation to think about the second discussion question, What can we do to fulfill this calling more fully? The answers to this question can be used to form new goals for the congregation.

## Strategy 3: Discover a Strength Gap

The third approach is to take a current strength of the congregation and help congregants see that this aspect of congregational life can become even stronger. With strength gaps an aspect of congregational life (such as worship music, pastoral care, or the youth program) that is considered by the congregation to be one of its best and most meaningful attributes becomes an attitude object. Congregations easily become content with strengths because they meet current needs and are sufficiently meaningful for people. But a gap can be created here when people can imagine the strength becoming more meaningful and helpful, not just to the current membership but also for others beyond the congregation. Strength gaps elicit pull motives for change, because people desire the benefits they will reap when congregational strengths become stronger. Consequently, the essential question of this strategy is, How can we become even better at doing what we already do well? Our church growth committee could have highlighted how people in our city were attracted to us because of our excellent music ministry and our strong seniors program. We could have asked the elders, "If people are already attracted to us by these two things, how can we make them even more meaningful and attractive?"

Here, the process called appreciative inquiry (often called AI for short) is excellent, since it is designed to help people imagine how to build on their organization's strengths.[5] The four-step process looks like this:

- *Discovery*: Articulate the organization's strengths and best practices, identifying "the best of what has been and what is." In other words, help congregants name and affirm the congregation's best attributes.
- *Dream*: Given these strengths, ask, "What are we being called to become?" In this step participants imagine the possibilities for building on the organization's strengths. The core task here is to "envision valued and vital futures."
- *Design*: Describe how your organization would look if it became what it was called to be. The core task here is to imagine what will be needed to attain and sustain the dream.

- *Destiny*: The core task of this step is to strengthen capability and context beliefs to strengthen hope and sustain positive momentum for change.[6]

Appreciative inquiry is a comprehensive process that engages the whole organization in positive and imaginative dialogue to create and achieve a vision for the future. The reader will note a modest degree of correlation between appreciative inquiry and the motivation-based process I describe in this book (even beyond our mutual affection for alliteration using words starting with the letter *d*). For the purposes of our discovery step, simply working through the first two AI steps— discovery and dream—are sufficient to create a discrepancy gap.

## Strategy 4: Discover an Identity Gap

The final approach reflects on the congregation's story. The stories congregants tell about themselves (such as "We are a friendly church" or "We always help people in need") convey and reaffirm important beliefs about the congregation, and along the way help maintain the status quo. But these beliefs can be out of alignment with "the facts" or how the congregation actually behaves. This approach to perceiving a discrepancy gap asks the essential questions, How does our congregational story today not reflect who we are in reality? and, Where do we fall short in living out our sense of identity? As in the first strategy, this approach makes the gap an attitude object for congregants and helps people form beliefs about the attitude object ("We aren't really the people we thought we were.") and to evaluate the attitude object negatively ("We need to change"). Identity gaps elicit push and pull motives for change.

Suppose my congregation thought of itself as friendly, welcoming, and hospitable. My church growth committee could have conducted some research, such as looking at the percentage of visitors who eventually made our congregation their church home. The committee could also have contacted those visitors who did not make our congregation their church home to ask them, "Why did you first attend? Why did you not return after that first visit?" We could also have contacted teens and young adults who grew up in the congregation but no longer attended to learn the reasons they left. The growth committee, through these surveys, might have learned that we did not exhibit the friendliness conveyed by people in their stories about our congregation. This kind of discrepancy gap calls the congregation's identity into question and fosters both push and pull motives. When a congregation's story affirms an attribute such as "We are a friendly church," congregants are naming a value that can become an aspiration and thus a pull motive. If congregants discover "We are not a friendly church," they can feel motivated to change their behavior so that it aligns better with their sense of identity. This is a push motive.

Leaders discover identity discrepancy gaps through listening (for how the congregation sees itself) and watching (for how the congregation behaves). Narrative leadership practices are perhaps the best way to discover both. People naturally conceive, carry, and communicate their sense of identity in story. They also naturally relate their behavior—especially past behavior—in story. Through facilitated gatherings or serendipitous conversations, leaders can discover where the congregational stories of identity differ from behavior.[7]

## Discrepancy Gaps, Cognitive Dissonance, and Change

An identity gap shows that something congregants believe about themselves is out of alignment with who they actually are, but the other three kinds of discrepancy gaps, in their own ways, can also challenge a congregation's identity. A current reality gap may imply that the congregation is not as fine, successful, or stable as people assume it is. An ideal-reality gap may imply that the congregation is not as faithful as people assume it is. A strength gap may imply that congregants set the bar too low when it comes to their understanding of strength.

Any gap may challenge a congregation's sense of identity or self-esteem, because a gap's existence disconfirms beliefs that the congregation held to be true about itself. These discoveries can foster dissatisfaction with the status quo, and dissatisfaction is a push motive for change. But discrepancy gaps can also foster another motivational force in people: cognitive dissonance. Cognitive dissonance is the discomfort we feel when we realize that our beliefs about ourselves do not align with our behavior or our reality in some way. This discomfort motivates us to reduce the gap so that the feeling of discomfort will disappear. We reduce the gap either by changing our behavior to align with what we believe about ourselves or by changing our beliefs to align them with how we wish to continue behaving. Once the gap is gone, so is the disconfirmation, since the congregation's behavior or reality aligns better with the congregation's beliefs about itself. This is the mechanism behind how discrepancy gaps create a degree of motivation for change. A congregation that discovers a discrepancy gap is taking the first step from precontemplation to contemplation, since the gap identifies the object of contemplation. If leaders can combine two approaches to discovery (such as helping people see both a current reality gap and an ideal-reality gap), then the motivational effect of the cognitive dissonance can become more powerful.

Change will not happen unless people first perceive some kind of discrepancy gap between how things are now and how things might be, but this means that people are likely to find some belief—and perhaps a cherished belief—about themselves disconfirmed. Consequently, helping people appreciate the existence of a discrepancy gap is serious and sensitive work that demands pastoral care. The disconfirmation the gap highlights can also weaken people's capability beliefs, because they may begin to question their ability to deal with the discrepancy gap. Disconfirmation can also raise the specter of loss—often because external locus of control beliefs result in congregants believing that their changing context will prevent them from reducing the discrepancy gap and return to a state in which their reality again reflects their beliefs about themselves. Leaders can mitigate the challenges that discrepancy gaps present to people in seven different ways:

- Acknowledge people's feelings publicly with compassion.
- Help people put their feelings into perspective by pointing out how other aspects of their congregation's life continue unchanged and well.
- Remind congregants of what is important in the grand scheme of things, which can again help people put their concern for the discrepancy gap into better perspective.
- Keep the process of change moving. People feel heartened when they see an issue addressed and progress made.

- Foster stronger context beliefs by helping congregants appreciate where their context does have an impact and where it does not.
- Help congregants regain stronger capability beliefs so that congregants appreciate how they can deal with the discrepancy gap.
- Continue to express the three qualities that inspire trustworthiness: benevolence, ability, and integrity. Maintaining and strengthening trust conveys care and helps support congregants as they move into the dialogue step.

When some people see a discrepancy gap, they instantly move into problem-solving mode in order to fix things. Moving immediately to fixing, however, preempts attitude change. Since the shift from precontemplation to contemplation holds the greatest promise for attitude change, this step needs time. In the discovery step, people need time to do exactly that: discover. A discrepancy gap provides a natural prompt to reflect on the origins, nature, and consequences of the gap, leading to questions such as, How was this gap created? Is the gap increasing? What impact does this discrepancy gap have on our current and future life as a congregation? Reflecting on a discrepancy gap can also cause congregants to evaluate their attitudes, through questions such as, How does our congregation perpetuate this gap? Why have we not noticed it before? What does it mean to us? and, Is it important enough to act on? When people start asking evaluative questions like these about a discrepancy gap, they are reconsidering their attitudes. If people proceed to fixing without attitude change, then chances are that old attitudes will prevail, and the discrepancy gap may well reemerge as a consequence.

So once a congregation has had some beliefs about its life disconfirmed by a discrepancy gap, leaders have the opportunity to help people reconsider and change their attitudes. Understanding the anatomy of an attitude is very useful at this point because it indicates the different places attitude change can take place:

- Attitudes start with a belief about an attitude object. If people change their belief about the issue at the core of a discrepancy gap, then the attitude will change.

- Attitudes contain an evaluation of the attitude object: that the belief is true or false, right or wrong, good or bad. When the evaluation changes, the attitude changes. An issue that was once evaluated as being OK could be reevaluated as being not OK.
- Similarly, people can come to hold attitudes more strongly, which will give the attitudes greater priority over others they have.
- Finally, an attitude can motivate action that depends on another evaluation: act or don't act, approach or avoid. When this motivational evaluation changes, the attitude changes.

Influencing any of these changes in attitudes can help congregants share enough common attitudes with sufficient strength that a group will develop a common intention to act. Let's examine each of these paths to attitude change.

## Changing the Beliefs of Attitudes

Studies have shown that the most effective means of encouraging attitudinal change is by helping people change their beliefs about an attitude object.[8] We come to our beliefs by one of three learning processes: by gaining new information from a source beyond ourselves, through an experience, or by thinking through an issue.

### Strategy 1: Provide New Information about the Belief

The most common strategy leaders use to encourage attitudinal change is to provide new information about an issue. In this approach, a leader analyzes what people believe about the attitude object, looks for the "facts" people use to support their belief, and then seeks to change the belief by providing different facts that disconfirm the current beliefs of congregants. For example, congregants can believe that all Presbyterian congregations sing exclusively traditional hymns. If a new fact is presented—such as, half of all Presbyterian congregations now sing contemporary praise songs as well—it can call the original belief into question.

Another information-based approach is to go about changing the facts themselves. An example of this approach is found in chapter 2, the story about the majority of St. Andrew's Church not wanting to construct an addition to the building. The facts were that the congregation ran annual deficits, had an outstanding and growing debt, had no experience with major fund-raising projects, had too many conflicting big-price-tag goals, and so on. In response, the leaders put the building program on hiatus for eighteen months so that these facts could be changed. Dispensing with these issues created new facts that fostered new beliefs, which in turn created new attitudes, so that people were keen on constructing the addition.

A funny part of human nature is that sometimes our willingness to adopt new beliefs depends on the messenger rather than the message. It has long been known that people take a message more seriously when someone they know and fully trust delivers it. A respected elder of the congregation delivering the facts of the situation can be far more influential than the lesser known convener of the committee set up to study the situation. Similarly, information coming from a reputed and respected expert can also influence beliefs. For example, in the mid-1970s, the congregation of my youth established its first long-range planning committee. For a few years the committee reported annually on membership decline, the aging of the congregation's membership, and the need to adopt some attitudes and practices of the church growth movement. Things did not change. So, in 1981 the renowned church consultant Lyle Schaller was invited by the board to study the congregation and make recommendations. The assessment and recommendations that Schaller made at a large congregational dinner were essentially what the congregation's own long-range planning committee had been saying for years. But for the congregation, hearing this assessment from North America's preeminent expert on congregation life was like hearing it for the first time. Schaller's message was influential in ways the committee could never have been.[9] The credibility of new information increases with the trust people have in the messenger.

## Strategy 2: Provide New Experiences about the Belief

A less common but very powerful strategy for changing beliefs is through providing opportunities for people to have new experiences. I used this approach to introduce projection for Sunday worship at St. Andrew's. Every four to six weeks for several months, I made it my habit to project images, words to hymns, and other text on an overhead screen, with the sole purpose of leaving people with positive impressions about it. I did not ask for permission in advance for this infrequent but regular divergence from our habit. The experience over ten months or so fostered positive attitudes among the majority of congregants. At that point, I proposed that we move to weekly implementation of projection, and the proposal was readily accepted. The experience provided a basis for a positive evaluation of using projected images and text in worship, which in turn formed new attitudes. The outcome may have been very different had I posed the question to the leaders before their seeing projection in action, since they would only have existing attitudes to govern their decision.

Another strategy for creating experiential learning opportunities is through practicing *creative deviance*. People notice a deviance from normal behavior, and that experience can cause people to think. The most dramatic example I've experienced of creative deviance was at a wedding ceremony I helped to conduct . . . with a Roman Catholic priest in his church. As we were putting on our robes before the service, the priest gave me and my blue Genevan gown a long and thoughtful look. Then he said, "When I get to the Mass, please come up and receive the host." I raised my eyebrows in surprise because I was aware that his suggestion was contrary to normal practice. "I want to send my congregation a message," he said. At the service, I was publicly introduced as the bride's pastor—a Presbyterian—and welcomed to share in the wedding ceremony. When the time for the communion distribution arrived, I joined the long line with the other parishioners, still wearing my Presbyterian best, and I can tell you that every pair of Roman Catholic eyes were opened wide as they followed my slow progress to the chancel, where I did receive the host. I can only imagine the conversation among the Catholics at the reception! But in that one simple act, the priest made a huge statement: the body of Christ is broader than just the Roman Catholic Church, and we should all embrace this truth. The congregants' experience of seeing their very own priest demonstrate this belief, in one small act of creative deviance that lasted only a few minutes, would have prompted much more thoughtful reflection than any sermon on the topic ever could.

Another way to engender experiential learning is something I call "let old dogs do old tricks," by which congregants disprove a belief by failing to prove it. Let's say after the economic downturn in late 2008, a congregation experienced a decline in financial support from its people. The tried-and-true response in the past when giving was down was the appeal from the pulpit, because "when our people know the need, they always respond." Even though the situation was different because of people's investment losses, mortgage worries, and fears of job loss, the historic attitude could well have prevailed. In such situations, a congregational leader may be wasting her time trying to argue that the old response won't work in the current situation. After all, the historic evidence behind the belief is that an appeal from the pulpit always works because it always worked! In a situation like this, people frequently need new, hard evidence that disconfirms their belief. Rather than argue against the appeal, however, a leader agrees to it—but with a question, "Yes, it has always worked, but given the economic situation today, will it work now?" This question plants the seed for a new belief. If the appeal doesn't have the expected result, then the old belief has been discredited by experience. The question raised by the leader may now become the new belief: that today's economic situation has had an impact on congregational finances. The disconfirmation of the old belief and the provision of a new potential belief can help people appreciate that it's now time for "old dogs to learn new tricks."

## Strategy 3: Provide Opportunities to Rethink Beliefs

As we saw in chapter 2, attitudes can function routinely to provide shortcuts for people's thinking about beliefs. Leaders can prompt people to rethink a belief by placing a roadblock in the midst of the shortcut. For example, if you hear an attitude expressed (such as, "Our congregation is doing OK"), you can intervene by asking, "Why do you think that?" This simple question acts as a roadblock to habitual thinking and forces a detour in thinking. The question causes a person to think consciously about his or her attitude and invites the person to share the belief that created the attitude (such as, "Well, worship attendance has been holding steady"). You can continue the intervention by challenging the belief: "But is that really true?" Now you are asking the person to consider the accuracy of the supposed evidence for the belief. You can also help people challenge their own belief by drawing attention to different evidence (such as, "Does our financial situation suggest that our congregation is doing OK?"). The goal of this kind of intervention is to interrupt habitual thinking, and the interruption provides an opportunity for people to rethink a belief and perhaps form a new attitude. Often you will find people are surprised to be asked to do this kind of thinking and surprised as well by what it reveals. In effect, you are helping people disconfirm their own beliefs, which they have probably held habitually and uncritically for some time.

In addition to interrupting people's habitual thought processes, leaders can also guide people through a thought process to rethink beliefs. An excellent format for people to use to reflect on their attitudes in faithful ways is the praxis method developed by Boston College professor Thomas Groome. This dialogue-based process helps people reflect critically on their past, their calling in faith, and their future. The process has five "movements":[10]

- *Name Present Practice.* For our purposes, the facilitator names an issue to be considered. Participants begin by describing how the issue is understood and perhaps lived out currently in the life of the congregation. They can express their feelings and attitudes toward the issue. The goal of this first movement is to bring to consciousness what people understand about the issue and what it means to them.
- *Reflect on Present Action.* Participants next reflect critically on what was expressed in the first movement. The goal of this movement is to "bring participants to a critical consciousness of present praxis: its reasons, interests, assumptions, prejudices, and ideologies

(reason); its socio-historical and biographical sources (memory); its intended, likely, and preferred consequences (imagination)."[11] In this movement people reflect on their attitudes: what they believe about the attitude object, how they have evaluated their beliefs, and what, if anything, those beliefs have motivated them to do.

- *Reflect on the Christian Story.* The facilitator then helps participants recall stories and tenets of their faith that seem to pertain to the issue. In this movement, participants begin to think about how their understanding of faith helps them better understand the issue as well as their possible calling regarding the issue.

- *Appropriate the Christian Story to the Participants' Stories.* Participants bring their reflections from movements 2 and 3 into dialogue with each other. The facilitator asks how the stories and tenets of faith affirm, call into question, and perhaps call the congregation beyond its current understanding and practices. The goal of this movement is to help participants appreciate their current beliefs and consider replacing them with new beliefs. Facilitators of this process, then, should help people maintain their focus on their attitudes, perhaps by asking questions such as, How might we think about the this issue? and, If we were to live with a new attitude around this issue, how might our lives change? Imagining in concrete ways how changed attitudes can lead to changed behavior can encourage people to adopt new attitudes.

- *Decide to Adopt a New Attitude for Christian Living.* Groome concludes his praxis method with an invitation to participants to choose new ways to think and live. For our purposes, this fifth movement offers participants an opportunity to embrace a new attitude. But to truly embrace a new attitude people must also imagine new ways of living. Part of the commitment of this movement, then, can be to develop a vision for the congregation's future that will inspire congregants to act on their new beliefs and attitudes. Developing this vision is the work of the dialogue step.

I like this process because it reflects so much of the thinking of this chapter. The second movement helps people become aware of their attitudes, and of the beliefs and evaluations that make up their attitudes. The third movement creates an ideal-reality discrepancy gap, and the fourth movement provides the opportunity for participants to reflect on their attitudes regarding the issue in light of the gap. The final movement calls for developing intentions to act. I have applied this method in such varied settings as workshops, sermons, ordering lesson plans, and one-on-one discussions.

## Changing the Evaluations of Attitudes

Attitudes follow most directly from people's beliefs about the attitude object, so belief change is the best route to attitude change. But beliefs are not the only component of an attitude. Attitudes also encompass three kinds of evaluation: the basic attitude evaluation (true or false, right or wrong, good or bad), a motivational evaluation (act or don't act, approach or avoid), and attitude strength (not important or very important). Attitudes change when any of these evaluations change. People have reasons for the evaluations they make about a belief, so changing it requires new, credible, and influential reasons.

For example, a decade ago I presented to our denomination's annual national meeting a demographic study that forecasted a 20 percent membership decline for the following decade. Our denomination, like many, had been in slow, steady decline for four decades. Consequently, the attitude of people at that national meeting was probably "decline is happening (belief), but there is little need for action (evaluation)." The purpose of the demographic study was in part to incite action. But the report was met by silence: not a single question or comment was made on the report or its recommendations, which were all adopted quietly. The evidence was new and credible, but it was not influential, so there was little attitude change. Apparently, a 20 percent membership decline over a decade was not deemed urgent enough. Ten years later, the actual net membership loss was 21.3 percent. Participants at the last two national meetings of our denomination have expressed a much higher level of concern for the future, mostly because of that loss. Now, with a 30 percent or more net membership loss expected in our current decade, the sense of urgency has increased, which in turn has changed the way many people evaluate the belief that "decline is happening": in the basic evaluation ("it is true we are declining"), the motivational evaluation ("act"), and the attitude strength ("strong"). The point of the story is this: people need new and credible reasons if they are going to change the way they evaluate their beliefs, but the reasons must be relevant, important, and influential for them.

The simplest way to encourage people to change their evaluation of an attitude object or issue is by helping them change their sense of urgency about the belief or issue. Leaders can help people assign greater importance to the attitude object and appreciate the time sensitivity for dealing with the discrepancy gap. Leaders might propose three or four reasons for changing the evaluation of a belief (a few well-chosen reasons are more influential than a comprehensive list of reasons). To influence congregational attitudes, the reasons have to be meaningful to congregants in some way. I failed to provide meaningful reasons to influence attitude change with my report on the demographic study. I assumed that the right idea always wins and that the numbers spoke for themselves. I was wrong with both assumptions. What I should have done was present a scenario describing the impact of a 21 percent membership loss on our organization. The consequences of further decline would include the following:

- increased financial strain on small congregations, with increased closures of congregations
- greater stress for regional governing bodies as they deal with these congregations
- budget challenges at the national office, leading to the amalgamation of departments and reduction of staff
- budget challenges for our theological colleges
- reduced funds for mission work nationally and internationally

These consequences would have added significance to the forecast and provided reasons for people to change their attitude evaluations from "don't act" to "act."

Attitude strength is another important factor that has been found to moderate intentions.[12] It is related to the confidence a person has in what he or she believes about the attitude object, the importance of the attitude to a person, and a person's experience with the attitude object. When a congregation considers an issue, some people will have weak attitudes that will favor change. Leaders strengthen motivation by helping people hold these attitudes more strongly. Other people may have attitudes, weak or strong, that do not favor change. Leaders build motivation for change by helping these people reduce the strength of these attitudes. Recall the teeter-totter decisional balance between drivers and resisters that is needed to foster intentions to change. In some circumstances, leaders may need to change only the motivational weight of existing attitudes to encourage new intentions.

Weak attitudes are strengthened when people are presented with new evidence that reinforces how right, true, and important their attitudes are. Attitudes are strengthened when people hear that others—especially influential people—share their attitude. Having a new experience of the issue can also strengthen attitudes. For example, a person may believe it is important for people who have the means to help the poor, but this attitude may be abstract with weak strength. Volunteering for a day at the local homeless shelter can make the abstract idea more real to the person, causing the volunteer to hold that attitude more strongly. Leaders can also strengthen weak attitudes by helping people link these attitudes to core values of their faith. Generally, the more consistency there is between our values, our attitudes, and our behavior, the more confident we feel in ourselves. When people are confident about their sense of self, they are more inclined to believe their attitudes are right.

The same strategies apply to weakening strong negative attitudes. When people are presented with contrary evidence that puts into question a belief about an attitude object, the strength of the belief can be challenged and weakened. Attitude strength can weaken when people learn that influential others hold different attitudes toward the same object, causing people to think twice about their own judgment. An experience can weaken attitude strength. For example, the attitude that a person with alcoholism can bootstrap himself out of addiction can be challenged by talking to someone from Alcoholics Anonymous.

Finally, seeing that one's attitude is out of alignment with a core value of the Christian faith can cause a degree of ambiguity in one's sense of self, which may lead to an attitude becoming weaker. Note that these approaches are not changing attitudes necessarily, but weakening their strength. Attitudes can be motives, so they too can be straws in our bales. When our attitudes become weaker those straws are being pushed back into our bales. When strong attitudes that oppose change become weaker, it affects the decisional balance of all our attitudes and motives. In the end, motivation for change may not require people to change attitudes but only to change the strength of some of their attitudes relative to other attitudes.

## Preparing for the Dialogue Step

Discovery is not about setting goals, imagining visions, and making plans. It is simply a time to help people recognize that there is a discrepancy gap between how things are and how things could be, to consider their attitudes that relate to the gap, and to recognize that changes in some attitudes may be needed to eliminate the gap. The dissatisfaction and cognitive dissonance created by the discrepancy gap begin building motivation for change in a congregation. As attitudes change, the decisional balance between drivers and resisters moves more in favor of change, which adds further motivation. The next step—dialogue—is when people begin to imagine what action will be needed to close the gap by formulating goals or a vision. Before leaders shift from discovery to dialogue, however, a few considerations can help them prepare for the next step.

### Strategy 1: Articulate the Congregation's New Vantage Point

One reason people remain in the precontemplation stage is that they do not change their perspectives, frames of reference, or worldviews. When congregants discover a discrepancy gap and find their attitudes changing, the original perspective, frame of reference, or worldview changes, creating a new vantage point for looking at and understanding the congregation. This new vantage point also helps people begin to imagine goals. The new vantage point may also strengthen capability and context beliefs, because congregants are looking at their situation in new ways. People are not always aware, however, that their vantage point has changed and, consequently, they may not gain the full advantage of their new perspective, frame of reference, or worldview. Leaders can help congregants notice how their point of view has changed and guide congregants in utilizing their new perspective, which may result in deeper learnings about the discrepancy gap and further changes to attitudes.

## Strategy 2: Adopt Learning Goals

An irony inherent in this stage of the change process is that appreciating a real need for change can impose a barrier to change. The barrier arises from the tension between simultaneously realizing that change is now important and that you don't know how to become or do something different. The congregation can feel pushed to give up some aspect of the status quo while simultaneously hesitating to adopt unfamiliar ways. Put another way, change can mean laying aside a competency in old ways in order to enter an unwanted time of feeling incompetent while adopting new ways. To use discrepancy gap terms, concerns about how things are prompt action, but an inability to define how things could be or should be impedes action. The sudden realization that change is needed can result in a congregation feeling stuck.

Social psychologist Edgar Schein, now retired from the MIT Sloan School of Management, was the first to write about how these tensions inhibit change. He characterized the tension as an impasse between "survival anxiety" ("I must change") and "learning anxiety" ("I don't know what to become" or "I don't know how to change"). Schein described the dynamic between these two anxieties this way:

> If disconfirming data get through your denial and defensiveness, you feel either survival anxiety or guilt. You recognize the need to change, the need to give up some old habits and ways of thinking, and the necessity of learning new habits and ways of thinking. But the minute you accept the need to change, you also begin to

experience learning anxiety. The interaction of these two anxieties creates the complex dynamics of change.[13]

As a first-time parent I experienced this in a big way when we took our son Paul home from the hospital. Sheri and I were eager to embrace parenthood, but at the same time we felt terribly unprepared for it. With a great deal of trepidation, we said our farewells to the health-care workers who had been our professional support staff for the first three days of Paul's life, but it was clear we couldn't stay. After being home a week I threw a party for Sheri to mark the fact that Paul had survived our care through his first seven days. We were learning to be parents! Congregations can feel similar tensions between "We want this change" and "We don't know that we can change" in situations such as these:

- The well-loved minister enters a well-deserved retirement after thirty years' service.
- A major decline in income forces significant changes to congregational life.
- Two congregations are amalgamated, creating a new dynamic because their community is half-filled with strangers.
- The congregation experiences a divisive conflict.

In situations like these, congregations can feel like Dorothy upon her arrival in the Land of Oz: "Toto, we're not in Kansas anymore." You know you have to go forward, but you are unsure how to move.

Schein asserts that people will move forward only when survival anxiety ("I can't stay the same") is higher than learning anxiety ("I don't know what to do"), and the needed imbalance is best created by reducing the learning anxiety. When leaders encounter this barrier to change, they often try to motivate congregants by heightening the survival anxiety in a Chicken Little ("The sky is falling!") kind of way. This approach tends to make people feel even more squished between the two types of anxiety they feel, which in turn makes the barrier to change stronger.

If your congregation is experiencing this barrier, then set aside the move to the dialogue step for a time and help congregants reduce their learning anxiety by addressing "We don't know what to do." Lead congregants through one or more vicarious experiences in mastery as described in chapter 3. Look for example congregations that once were in your situation and successfully changed. Learn from these congregations directly through inquiry and discussion, or indirectly by reading books on the issue your congregation faces or by engaging a consultant. Vicarious experiences in mastery reduce learning anxiety in two ways. First, the experiences teach congregants that there are a number of ways to address their issue. These experiences will help them say "We do know what to do" and provide several viable options for consideration. Second, vicarious experiences in mastery increase capability beliefs, because congregants grow in the belief that "if those congregations could do it, then we can do it too!" When people appreciate that they have several viable options for moving forward and when they have stronger capability beliefs, the learning anxiety barrier to moving forward is reduced. This change opens the way to move into the dialogue step.

### Strategy 3: Find the Early Adopters

The early adopters begin to come into existence during discovery because they are the first to understand the discrepancy gap, have a sense of urgency to deal with the gap, and appreciate that changes in attitudes may be needed for change to take place. Early adopters become advocates for change, either by their own initiative or as a result of encouragement. Look for the emergence of early adopters during discovery. If encouraged to do so, they will assist in helping congregants understand the discrepancy gap and exemplify the new attitudes required for change to happen. The early adopters will also be needed during the dialogue step to foster the crucial discussions that influence the early majority to adopt new directions.

## Moving On to the Dialogue Step

Choosing when to move on to dialogue depends on the judgment of congregational leaders and their answers to questions such as these:

- Do congregants clearly understand the discrepancy gap?
- Have congregants been reevaluating their attitudes?
- Are congregants developing new perspectives, frames of reference, or worldviews that help them understand their congregation in new ways?
- Has there been sufficient change in attitudes to prepare congregants to formulate a vision or goals for the future?

As you move into the next step, remember that it is unlikely everyone in the congregation will make the move with you. The transtheoretical model and diffusion theory help us appreciate that everyone will not make the shift from precontemplation to contemplation at the same time. Consequently, during dialogue leaders will still be required to do the work of discovery for the sake of those still in the precontemplation stage, helping them to perceive and understand the discrepancy gap and to reevaluate their attitudes.

## CHAPTER 7

# Developing the Change Story Together: The Dialogue Step

*We talk all the time about changing minds. The meaning of this exceedingly common metaphor seems clear enough: we have a mind set in one direction, some operation is performed, and—lo and behold—the mind is now set in another direction. But minds, of course, are hard to change.*[1]
—Howard Gardner

In the dialogue step, congregants move from the contemplation stage to the preparation stage. The goal of this step is to help congregants develop an intention to change. During dialogue the discrepancy gap becomes clearer to congregants—making the push and pull motives more evident—and a direction for the future begins to emerge as the solution for reducing the gap. Hope for the future develops because the emerging direction will satisfy the motives favoring change and positive attitudes are formed toward the vision or goal. When congregants come to share enough common attitudes of sufficient strength, then they will develop a common intention to act. The role of leaders is to influence how people think about the emerging direction. This influence comes through dialogue. The word *dialogue* is formed from two Greek roots that mean "through" and "the word." Through the words of dialogue, people develop greater clarity about the discrepancy gap, stronger concerns and hopes, stronger motives, shared meaning, and stronger context and capability beliefs. Dialogue also potentially helps people learn how to think together and develop new shared perspectives, points of view, and worldviews. In other words, dialogue is a means for bringing about attitude change, which in turn enables congregational change.

Think of the purpose of the dialogue and deliberation (discussed in detail in chapter 8) steps as encouraging two parallel, growing movements in the congregation. In the first movement, congregants conceive, clarify, and formalize a direction for the future, which they may call a vision or a goal. The second movement is the coming together of the early majority, who favor the emerging direction. These two movements happen concurrently: as the vision becomes more clear and compelling, more people join the early majority. During dialogue, the first of the early majority coalesces around the emerging direction, because these individuals have been influenced by the discussions during this step and find the tentative direction appealing. The rest of the early majority is formed during deliberation, when congregants are influenced by the final, official vision that is communicated through a crafted change message. In other words, the first of the early majority is convinced to join the movement for change during dialogue, through the loose discussions that formulate the vision, but the rest of the early majority needs to be persuaded to join during deliberation. Taken together, dialogue and deliberation create a snowball effect. Leaders move from the dialogue to the deliberation step when a majority of the congregation appears to be part of the early majority. The deliberation step is meant to increase the size of the early majority even more. By the time leaders have worked through dialogue and deliberation, they can be confident that a good-sized majority of the congregation is prepared to adopt the vision formally.

## Vision Creation in a Culture of Choice

Peter Senge, a senior lecturer in leadership at the Sloan School of Management, outlined a spectrum of five different leadership approaches that move from minimum to maximum people involvement in developing a direction for the future:[2]

- Telling: Leaders create the vision by themselves and then say "This is the way it's going to be, so get on with it."
- Selling: Leaders create the vision by themselves, and then promote it in a way that gets people to buy into it.
- Testing: Leaders conceive an initial draft vision, share the draft with congregants to obtain feedback, and then improve the vision in light of the feedback.
- Consulting: Before creating a vision, leaders seek advice from stakeholders and key constituent groups to provide input for vision creation.
- Cocreating: Leaders work collaboratively with congregants from the beginning to create a shared vision together.

The amount of dialogue increases as one moves through the degrees of involvement, from *telling* to *cocreating*. As a general rule, the farther leaders move along this spectrum of involvement, the more people will embrace the final vision and be motivated to attain it, because more involvement leads to greater ownership of the final vision by more people. More engagement also helps leaders learn what will motivate congregants to commit to the vision and pursue it.

Some congregational leadership books suggest that *selling* or *testing* are really the way leaders normally engage with their congregations about change. But in our fully democratized, consumer-oriented, individualistic culture, leaders must ask whether the degree of congregational involvement in vision creation needs to be greater than may first be assumed. More dialogue and involvement is needed

- in congregations that are smaller,
- if the proposed change makes congregants anxious,
- when a change in the congregation's culture is required,
- when what is being proposed does not align with the congregation's current assumptions about the calling and nature of the faith community,
- when members assume that direction is determined democratically,
- when the polity is congregationalist,

- if the congregation is Roman Catholic or mainline Protestant,[3]
- in culturally diverse congregations,
- when generational differences are typically ignored in decision making,
- in low-commitment congregations, where enrolling people in a proposed direction may be difficult, and
- when the new direction will be out of step with a congregation's traditions and past history.

As a general rule, an increasing degree of involvement through dialogue will be needed as the impact of change increases and the expectation for participation in decision making increases.

## Dialogue, Vision, and the Change Message

In the deliberation step, which follows dialogue, a clearly defined goal or vision will be the focus of discussion. A change message will be crafted to present the rationale for the goal or vision and used to persuade congregants to affirm the proposed direction. The dialogue step helps leaders discover what the most motivating vision is and learn what will make the most persuasive change message. Dialogue is a precursor step, during which the vision and change message emerge simultaneously with one influencing the other as both become clearer.

Perhaps the most motivating vision for the congregation is not the most effective one or the preferred choice of the leaders, but the one most likely to be attained. Leaders can strengthen the motivational influence of the vision that emerges during dialogue using the seven characteristics of a well-crafted goal, found in chapter 2: the goal is specific, immediate, necessary, congruent with congregational identity, expressed in positive language, challenging, and clearly responsive to congregational motives. Dialogue helps leaders discover not only the most appealing direction but also how best to apply the seven characteristics of a well-crafted goal to make the goal most appealing to the congregation.

Dialogue also provides the opportunity to begin crafting the change message. As possible future directions emerge, congregants will discuss the pros and cons of each option. This discussion provides an excellent opportunity for leaders to learn the most common and important driver and resister motives and attitudes to be considered when creating the change message. Dialogue may also be an excellent time to conduct a force field analysis exercise to determine which drivers should be strengthened and which resisters weakened or even eliminated. Recall the story in chapter 2 about how this work was conducted at St. Andrew's Church in Calgary in preparation for a construction project. We extended the length of the dialogue step eighteen months in order to eliminate as many resisters as possible before moving on to the deliberation step.

## Fostering Congregational Dialogue

In some situations, the issues are easily understood and congregants quickly determine goals to address them. A congregation, for example, could see the number of working poor in their neighborhood and respond by opening a local food bank. Other situations are not so clear cut. For example, in the fall of 2010 our congregation's leaders were talking about new directions. We wanted to be good stewards of our congregation's future by acting well today for the sake of the congregation that will follow us. Then, unexpectedly, the following issues came before our congregation over a three-month period:

- Our regional governing body chose to amalgamate a smaller sister congregation into our congregation.
- The same governing body directed us to create what they called "a new ministry" in south Calgary and designated $1 million from the sale of the smaller church facility as a resource for the new ministry. The governing body provided no definition for what this new ministry should be.
- The neighboring YMCA closed, putting in jeopardy our access to their parking lot, which we had enjoyed for more than forty years.

- The administration of the city of Calgary asked us to
  consider selling our land and relocating to accommodate a
  development the city administration wished to see on the
  YMCA property.

The simple visioning work of the fall of 2010 suddenly became extremely complex, forcing us to ask some very big questions, such
as, Do we leave this location and become the new ministry in south
Calgary? These issues became the focus of dialogue over the next
sixteen months.

As I discussed in chapter 4, Harvard's Ronald Heifetz calls a situation like this an "adaptive challenge,"[4] which can only be addressed
through changes in an organization's culture: people's beliefs, values,
priorities, norms of behavior, and loyalties. An adaptive challenge
exists when the typical responses or fixes found in a congregation's
cultural repertoire cannot deal with the issue; rather, the culture must
adapt or evolve to meet the challenge.

Adaptive change requires stressful and at times conflictual dialogue,
so a container needs to be created in which to hold discussion. Heifetz
calls this a "holding environment."[5] A holding environment is created
when leaders direct and maintain congregants' attention to the issue
and facilitate discussion about the issue. The holding environment
is maintained by regulating the stress of the discussion. Within this
holding environment leaders help congregants collect and understand
information pertaining to the issues, moderate discussions, and then
frame and reframe the issue in light of the information at hand. In a
faith community setting, the holding environment should be understood as a sacred space: the meeting place for faith-filled people seeking
a faithful response to their issue, where people can be encouraged to
treat each other with respect.

Heifetz also recommends five "strategic principles of leadership"
for facilitating the discussions within the holding environment:

1. *Identify the adaptive challenge.*[6] Name what the issue is,
   which is defined (in the terms of this book) by the discrepancy gap. Help congregants through dialogue to understand
   what has created the issue, what the issue puts at stake in

congregational life, and what the congregation needs to learn to address the challenge.

2. *Keep the level of distress within a tolerable range for doing adaptive work.*[7] By maintaining sufficient urgency for the dialogue, the leader ensures people will maintain their focus on the issue. If there is too little urgency, people will not engage the issue. If there is too much urgency and stress in discussion, people can feel overwhelmed, and they will not learn new ways if they are overwhelmed.

3. *Focus attention on ripening the issue.*[8] Heifetz says that an "unripe issue" is one that captures the attention of only a small minority of a community, which is an insufficient nucleus for dialogue if an adaptive challenge is going to be addressed. An issue is ripe when the attention of a significant portion of a community is focused on it with enough urgency to prompt dialogue.[9] A work of leadership, then, is to ripen issues and broaden discussion. Focused attention on the issue over time is also needed, so leaders must not let distractions interrupt or derail dialogue. As Heifetz writes, "Attention is the currency of leadership. Getting people to pay attention to tough issues rather than diversions is at the heart of strategy."[10]

4. *Give the work back to the people, but at a rate they are able to stand.*[11] An adaptive challenge can be met only by a change in culture, which cannot be imposed on people. If leaders give congregants the work of determining how the congregation should evolve—while providing the holding environment for dialogue, help for maintaining focus on the issue, and regulating congregants' distress as they consider change—then congregants can come to their own solutions to the issue. Dialogue such as this takes time. Congregants also need time to truly appreciate the issue and what is at stake. They also need time to recognize and accept their responsibility to deal with the issue. A congregation jumping into sensitive, potentially life-changing issues too quickly is in as much danger as a nonswimmer jumping into a pool's deep end. The congregation must be supported on its journey toward the real issues, paced in a way that allows congregants to cope.

5. *Protect the voices of the emerging leadership.*[12] As dialogue
   ensues, the analysis and proposals of some congregants will
   gain traction in the congregation. These people will need encouragement, affirmation, support, and perhaps even defense
   in order for their voices to be heard and their ideas considered.

Heifetz's five strategic principles of leadership were used to encourage
and guide dialogue for the board of St. Andrew's Church as it dealt
with its complex issues. The adaptive challenge (strategic principle 1),
on the surface, appeared to be a collection of individual tasks: find a
solution to our parking dilemma, define what we wanted to do in a
new ministry in south Calgary, respond to the city's request to relocate,
and through it all be good stewards of the future of our congregation.
As we considered these tasks, however, it became apparent that they
were not necessarily independent one from another. For example,
we quickly realized that we could become the new ministry in south
Calgary through relocation and solve our parking problem at the
same time. We also saw that solving one issue could make dealing
with another issue more difficult. For example, if we created a second
campus for our congregation in south Calgary, would we irreparably
weaken our current congregation and put its future in jeopardy?
Would we be good stewards of our future if we took this direction?
The board appreciated that we faced an adaptive challenge, since
anything we did would require cultural change, whether that was as
big as relocating a congregation of one thousand people or as small
and seemingly straightforward as the task of helping people change
their parking habits.

Learning became the important first step to understand the real
nature of the adaptive challenge before us. We came up with a collection of questions that needed answers:

- What was the city planning to develop on the YMCA
  property—and potentially on our property? Would it
  be best if we relocated, partnered with the city in the
  development, or just stayed and lived with the consequences
  for our parking? A team made up of capable people was

created to help us understand our options regarding these issues.

- What would be our new mission in south Calgary? Would it be planting a new, independent congregation or creating a second campus for our congregation? Would it be a social ministry? Could it be some combination of these options? The board needed a feasibility study to help it understand the congregational option. The board also sought input from congregants who were professionals working every day in a variety of contexts meeting social needs.

- Who would form the next generation of St. Andrew's Church? What was the emerging generation like? What do they look for in a church? What do they find meaningful? What are their needs? In other words, what might we have to do today to ensure we are good stewards of our future? The two ministers of St. Andrew's helped the board learn more about the emerging generation.

The level of distress was maintained within a tolerable and productive range (strategic principle 2) in a few different ways. First, we resolved to deal with the relocation issue according to our time frame, rather than be driven only by city-imposed deadlines. That choice preempted a sense of panic, put us more in control of our destiny, and relieved some stress. We were also acutely aware of the responsibility we held for the mandate given us by our regional governing body, toward the people of the congregation now amalgamated into us who entrusted us with their assets, and for the well-being of our congregation today and tomorrow. Finally, remembering that the ongoing permission to park on the YMCA lot could be withdrawn at any time maintained a sense of urgency. The board regulated the congregation's possible distress over the parking plight by not making public the possibility of selling our property and moving. We did not want to create a panic by announcing that the city essentially gave us a four-month deadline to consider selling our property. Once the board determined that there was no net benefit to relocation, it informed the congregation of the city's proposal and the board's decision to reject it. The congregation was surprised by the revelation and relieved by the response.

Given Heifetz's definition that an issue is ripe when a significant portion of a group is focused on the issue with a sense of urgency to deal with it (strategic principle 3), the issues facing our board were ripe from the very beginning. Having four big issues presented to us suddenly and concurrently prompted immediate action. Given the significance of the issues the board was working on, the ministers ensured that the board's main focus over the eighteen months remained primarily on the task of dealing with these issues and that it not be distracted by others. Fortunately, the board was already organized in a way that forty-five to sixty minutes of each meeting was always allocated to discuss an issue of importance.

As for the congregation, it was important to ripen the issue of a new ministry in south Calgary. Congregants were informed from the beginning about the mandate to create a new ministry in south Calgary. They were asked at a congregational meeting to affirm in principle a commitment to pursue some new form of ministry for south Calgary, and they agreed. Congregants were also invited to provide suggestions for the form of that ministry, but few came in. The leaders found that understandable, since there was virtually nothing to focus thoughts or discussion, and congregants perceived little urgency to help at this initial stage. The board decided to provide leadership in vision creation, and over time, it used two of Senge's methods to involve people in the discussion. When a vision began to emerge about what the board was calling family ministry (which will be described later), a consultative process was undertaken to elicit input for the idea. As the vision for family ministry took greater shape, the idea was tested on the congregation as a whole. Our congregation is organized into sixty-five districts, each composed of eight to ten households, with a member designated to be a liaison and to offer pastoral care to those in his or her district. Through this organization, we managed to hold personal conversations with most of our congregants. The results of those conversations, in turn, helped the leaders fine-tune the change message so that it addressed motives, concerns, and questions more effectively. The final version of the vision was presented to the congregation in February 2013 and was adopted unanimously.

Throughout this prolonged period of dialogue, the ministers had their own opinions on the best direction for our congregation's future, but they were never presented to the leaders. Honestly, our preference was only one of several potential directions, and who was to say that our preference was the best. At times some leaders sought our opinion, but we resisted providing it because we believed the work of addressing an adaptive challenge must be given back to the people (strategic principle 4) if the new direction requires a change in congregational culture. After all, if we are going to do something dramatic, then the congregation as a whole has to fully own the direction.

Sixteen months of dialogue by the board resulted in the broad strokes of a vision for a social ministry aimed at meeting needs of families in south Calgary. Our hope is that this ministry as an expression of loving our neighbor will build credibility and respect for the Christian faith and lead to developing a worshiping community as a second campus of St. Andrew's Church. This was the bare-bones vision adopted by the congregation, but the dialogue work is far from over. The work of choosing the nature of the social ministry will be given to the congregation as a whole, since the choice of ministry will have to be sufficiently appealing and meaningful to motivate maximum involvement.

As you can see, the dialogue step can take a prolonged period of time, depending on how significant the adaptive challenge is. Dialogue takes patience, because every birth is preceded by a gestation period, and that period cannot be rushed. Engaging in direction setting is not only about casting a vision for the future. It is also about developing the widest consensus possible for the most motivating vision so that people who live in a culture of choice will give the vision their enthusiastic "Yes!"

## Creating Vision through Story

So, how should congregational leaders facilitate dialogue so that the process feels natural for participants and, in the end, is productive? What form should dialogue take? Leaders may choose a highly structured, facilitated format or leave discussion loose and freewheeling. Some leaders may prefer a technical discussion filled with facts and figures. Another alternative, however, is a process rooted in narrative.

New York University's Jerome Bruner left a mark on psychology by providing a comprehensive theory on the narrative construction of reality. In essence, he argues that through the autobiography we construct and tell ourselves, we make sense of our past experience and shape our future life experience. As Bruner puts it, "In the end, we *become* the autobiographical narratives by which we tell about our lives."[13] Humans tell themselves into their future existence through self-narrative.

This idea suggests three applications for understanding a congregation and envisioning its future. First, the stories congregants tell about their congregation provide rich insight into their culture, the common attitudes and motives for acting, as well as the tacit functional goals they hold for the future, which are all very helpful for leaders as they analyze their congregation. But Bruner suggests that these stories of a congregation's past and present also determine how its future will unfold. If congregations are to change, then congregants need to imagine and embrace a new storyline for the future they want to pursue.

Second, we imagine our future in the form of stories, which typically take the form of scenarios. A scenario is a specific story form that describes the future based on one or a few assumptions about what the future will be like. We can imagine the future unfolding in multiple ways, depending on different variables. Not all these alternative futures are agreeable, so we hope and work for our preferred choice. Leadership books often say that a vision for the future must be "richly imagined" and "compelling." A well-storied vision can be both these things and become the future that congregants want to tell into existence.

Third, we describe the journey to our preferred future through a storyline. These storylines often take the form of "the hero's journey," which Joseph Campbell called an archetypal myth.[14] Notice how the following description of the hero's journey sounds much like the story of congregational change. Heroes leave their habitual life and embark on a journey into an unfamiliar world, often in response to some calling. There is something to gain through the quest, which is filled with tasks and challenges. Successful heroes obtain the object of their quest:

a prize. If the heroes choose to return home, then the prize becomes a boon to their community and improves its life. A plan that takes a congregation from its current reality to the attainment of its vision often echoes this archetype. Imagining change as an unfolding story helps people understand *how* (in Bruner's terms) to tell their desired future into existence. As people richly imagine the tasks and challenges of their quest, they learn what needs to be included in their objective plans for goal attainment.

If Bruner is correct that humans are narrative beings who use story to make sense of reality and to tell their future into existence, then approaching vision creation in a narrative way is probably helpful to people. The following questions can encourage congregants to share their storylines about the congregation's past, current situation, anticipated futures, and preferred future. The progression of the questions follows the same pattern of the praxis method of Thomas Groome that I outlined in chapter 6.

- How are things today for our congregation?
- How has our congregation's past contributed to our current reality? What stories of our past illustrate this connection?
- What will be our most likely future if our current storyline is allowed simply to unfold?
- What is God's mission in our world today, and how could God's story influence the unfolding of our story?
- Given our story thus far and what God wants for the world, what might be the preferred storyline for moving into our future?

Leaders may use these questions simply to envision a congregation's direction, but attentiveness to the stories elicited by the questions will also provide insights into congregational motivation. Recall that the purpose of dialogue is to help congregants develop intentions to change, which are created when driver motives and attitudes outweigh resister motives and attitudes in congregants' minds. Let's look at how these questions can be used to learn more about what will motivate a congregation.

## Tell the Past and Present Story

The first questions are closely related and can be dealt with together: How are things today for our congregation? How has our congregation's past contributed to our current reality? What stories of our past illustrate this connection?

People's stories of their congregation, like the stories of the Bible, contain motives and reflect attitudes, both past and present. "The worship service here reminds me of the worship I grew up with as a child" may reflect a favorable attitude toward the current style of worship. "You hear all the time about churches declining, but ours is doing just fine" may reflect an attitude that is resistant to change. "Church is no longer a priority for families today" may well express low capability and context beliefs, which would diminish any hope that the congregation could successfully reach out again to younger families. "We've always focused more on what we do for ourselves and focused little on what we do for others" may indicate the presence of a push motive to engage more in mission. Asking *why* questions about the stories people tell helps them consider motives and attitudes, as well as encourages them to explore their concerns.

## Imagine the Likely Future Scenario

The next question to ask is, What will be our most likely future if our current storyline is allowed to unfold? No one knows what the future holds, and yet many people think they have a pretty good idea. Their ideas are based on their attitudes: their beliefs about what is happening now, their evaluations of those beliefs, and the future scenario that is the most logical consequence of their beliefs and attitudes. People will view their future storylines positively or negatively, and either viewpoint may motivate intentions for action or inaction. Leadership, in part, is about helping people feel moved into action by their point of view, whether it is positive or negative.

For example, in my own congregation, we have people who describe very positive stories of our congregation's future. They believe our congregation is growing and that new young families are joining us who are attracted by our congregation's many strengths. These congregants see a trajectory of a positive storyline into our future because of the beliefs and evaluations they have regarding our current life. Of this group some hold the attitude that maintaining the status quo is the best response to our current reality, since "whatever we're doing is working." For others the same positive future storyline motivates action, because they hope to see even more young families come to our church, and this desire is for them a pull motive.

Others at St. Andrew's observe our current reality differently and thus have a different view of the future. They note that our church school is smaller than it was during the golden age of the baby boom. On Sunday morning they see the significant number of older adults whose habits are to attend weekly, compared to members of the younger generation, who are less regular in worship attendance. The beliefs and evaluations of these people foster a negative view of our future—one of decline. But again, this negative future scenario may prompt action in some people and inaction in others. Low capability and context beliefs often foster defeatist attitudes that immobilize people because they believe their current reality is inescapable. For others the same negative future scenario prompts concern, which becomes a push motive.

People's scenarios for the congregation's future say much about beliefs and attitudes regarding current reality. Both positive and negative scenarios can motivate and demotivate. Rather than attempt to change people's point of view, leaders may find it simpler and more effective to help people feel moved to act on their point of view, whatever it is. Those with a positive view of the future can be encouraged to build on present strength, and those with a negative view of the future can be encouraged not to let the storyline they imagine become their destiny.

## Imagine God's Story

The next question to consider is, What is God's mission in our world today, and how could God's story influence the unfolding of our story? Imagining that the purpose of a congregation is to align itself with the *missio Dei* may be an unfamiliar perspective for congregants, but looking at familiar things in new ways often leads to new insights.

Spending time in discernment with congregants about God's purposes and work in the congregation's current context generates four insights. First, discernment is a way to reflect on the congregation's understanding of the nature and callings of the faith community leading to renewed beliefs, priorities, and practices, which typically make involvement in the faith community more meaningful. Second, it helps people imagine and articulate visions for the future, which provide a focus for hope and give people something to desire and anticipate. Third, this discussion strengthens a congregation's sense of stewardship. If God is pursuing the *missio Dei*, then God would be pleased to entrust to coworkers part of that work. Finally, it strengthens capability beliefs. After all, people are helping the God of the universe with what God is doing.

## Narrate the Congregation's Preferred Future

Given the story thus far, and what God wants for the world, what might be the preferred storyline for moving into our future? This question invites people to envision their preferred future in light of the stories told thus far. Imagining a direction that holds wide appeal in a congregation is certainly the best outcome of this process. But it is not the only outcome that leaders should seek. Asking the question, Why is this hoped-for future important to you? reveals motives and attitudes that favor change as well as the motives and attitudes for not pursuing the emerging vision. Knowing both collections of motives and attitudes will be important for creating a preliminary draft of a vision, to which we now turn.

## The Draft Vision

Unless a fully collaborative process has been used, it will fall upon the leaders to prepare a first draft of the vision based on what is learned through dialogue to this point. In drafting a vision for the future, the goal is not just to describe a direction but also to understand and articulate what will motivate people to choose that direction. With the draft vision in view, leaders can ask questions such as these:

- What are the most prevalent attitudes that favor this vision? What are the push and pull motives underlying those attitudes? How widespread and strong are these motives?
- What prevailing attitudes would not favor this vision? What are the motives underlying those attitudes? How widespread and strong are these motives?
- What has this process taught us about the capability and context beliefs of congregants? Do these beliefs need strengthening?
- How is the balance between drivers and resisters? What might we have to do to tilt the balance more strongly in favor of drivers?

Force field analysis is the method of choice for answering these questions. Congregants will have many motives that will encourage or resist change. Recall also that attitudes are preevaluations and predecisions, so it is important to assess at this early stage how current attitudes are also lining up as drivers and resisters for the emerging vision. Drivers need to outweigh resisters before leaving the dialogue step. If you find that the resisters outweigh the drivers, then you will need to return to the discovery step to encourage changes in attitude. Moving back a step, if needed, should not be seen in any way as failure, since a primary purpose of a draft vision is to give leaders an opportunity to consider prevailing attitudes and motives in a different light, bringing new insights. Besides, according to the transtheoretical model, the trajectory of change is not always forward but often requires circling back in order to make headway.

Everything leaders have learned to this point contributes to goal setting or vision creation. The more the draft vision reflects congregants' push and pull motives for change, the more that vision will be compelling. In addition, because the draft vision articulates the concerns, hopes, and motives of congregants, congregants will not perceive it as the independent idea of the leaders that needs to be "sold." Rather, the draft vision will feel like the heart of congregants echoed back in a well-articulated way. Of course, some scenarios for the future of your congregation will be more right than others, and the leaders' role will be to determine which vision that is. But chances are that among the potential directions, the direction congregants find most appealing and motivating will be viewed as the right idea by the majority of congregants.

## The Early Majority and Early Adopters

As an issue becomes more apparent and relevant to people, prompting concern, they consequently become more apt to notice the issue and think and talk about it.[15] Dialogue encourages discussion about the past, present, and future as well as acts of diagnosis, discernment, and direction setting. The invitation to enter dialogue is, in its own way, a change message because the invitation implies that change may be needed. Participation in dialogue creates opportunities for congregants to hear additional change messages from their various partners in discussion. Such communications are important to the early majority because this group is marked by their need to discuss changes with others before adopting an innovation. Among the influences on the early majority are the congregation's opinion leaders, who help to prompt dialogue. There are two kinds of opinion leader: the early adopters of the innovation and the traditional opinion leaders of the congregation. A change effort is assisted immensely when a number of opinion leaders of both these kinds favor a new direction.

Early adopters become opinion leaders by virtue of being the first to adopt an emerging vision for the future. During discovery, they will be among the first to understand the discrepancy gap. Indeed, they may have perceived the gap during precontemplation and begun even then to imagine ways to respond to the gap. When early adopters are asked to participate in a process to envision the future they will likely be the ones who are most keen and diligent to do so. Encouraging early adopters to take their awareness, understanding, and attitudes with them into conversation with others will both capture their motivated behavior and help them become opinion leaders. They become what Rogers calls a "diffusion network." Early adopters, by their very nature, are primed to be able opinion leaders. They only need encouragement to do so.

Traditional opinion leaders are different from early adopters (although some may become early adopters). Traditional opinion leaders often have an influence in any issue in a congregation because of congregants' respect for them. Traditional opinion leaders have a sphere of influence, which may be the entire congregation, those who participate in a congregational activity, or their personal friendship circles. Traditional opinion leaders, by their nature, tend to watch what is happening in their congregation and form and share their attitudes on emerging visions for the future. The respect opinion leaders have in their own circles adds substantial credibility to the change message . . . if they become proponents of the vision.

During dialogue, wise leaders seek out the traditional opinion leaders and invite their insights regarding the discrepancy gap and emerging vision for the future. People who contribute to a new direction generally have more ownership of it and become more avid advocates for it. Encouraging opinion leaders who favor the emerging vision to be a part of the congregation's dispersed discussion on the issue is also valuable. Perhaps they will also be willing to report back on how the talk about the issue is unfolding in congregational life. Leaders need to know how the idea of change is being accepted and whether the size of the early majority is growing. This feedback also helps leaders appreciate what drivers and resisters are most influential for congregants, which will be critical both for further interventions promoting attitude change and for crafting the official change message.

## Influencing Opinion Leaders
## Who May Not Favor Change

Some traditional opinion leaders may not see the discrepancy gap as important or may disagree with the emerging direction for the congregation. Such people need to be taken seriously, because within their spheres of influence, other congregants believe these opinion leaders provide wise counsel. The group leading the change effort may well benefit from their insights, which may result in an improved direction for the congregation's future. A conversation with opinion leaders who disagree may also help them embrace the direction. Opinion leaders who convert often have significant influence on those in their spheres of influence, because the factors that helped the opinion leaders change their minds are equally influential to their "near peers." There are three ways leaders are able to influence traditional opinion leaders who disagree with an emerging vision for the future: one-on-one conversations, inviting opinion leaders to meet with the leaders for the new initiative, and focus groups that mix opinion leaders who hold a variety of opinions regarding the emerging direction. Let's explore each of these three strategies in turn.

## Strategy 1: One-on-One Discussion

A basic tenet in social psychology is that people's commitment to a position will increase as they argue in favor of that position. The counseling approach called motivational interviewing applies this idea with a twist: a person who disagrees with the emerging vision is led to reflect on the merits of the emerging vision. A conversation guided by the motivational interview process works through four sequential steps.

Step 1: Help people articulate from their own perspective what they think are the disadvantages of the status quo, which will clarify their own understanding of how the current reality in their congregation is detrimental in some way. Step 1 assists people in recognizing their own personal push motives in favor of change.

Step 2: Ask people to name what they think are the advantages of the emerging direction. By naming advantages, people recognize their own personal pull motives in favor of change. These first two steps together help people describe the discrepancy gap in their own terms.

Step 3: Invite people to assess, from their perspective, the congregation's capacity to attain the emerging goal. In other words, help people articulate their capability and context beliefs about the congregation.

Step 4: Assist people in developing an intention to change by weighing their own motives identified in the first two steps against their initial reasons for not changing. Help people find a new balance between their own drivers and resisters.

To be effective in this approach, congregational leaders must demonstrate respect for these opinion leaders and acceptance of them despite their contrary opinions. By showing respect and empathy for their feelings and seeking to understand them and their issues without criticizing, judging, or blaming, leaders will honor their choices. In general, people who are accepted even in their differences are more apt to consider change. This approach enacts the prayer of St. Francis, "O Divine Master, grant that I may not so much seek . . . to be understood as to understand."

## Strategy 2: A Meeting with Opinion Leaders

Conversation between the leadership group that favors change and opinion leaders who disagree with the emerging direction is mutually beneficial. Thinking again of Senge's leadership approaches for involving people in planned change, leaders can talk to opinion leaders early on during dialogue to gain their wisdom (*consulting*) or later during dialogue to gather their opinions concerning the emerging vision for the future (*testing*). Conversations like these may lead to modifications in the emerging vision with which the opinion leaders could agree.

Leaders may be tempted in such encounters simply to advocate the emerging vision, hoping that a solid rational argument in favor of the new direction will convince these people to change their minds. Harvard psychologist Howard Gardner argues for a very different approach. Leaders, rather than arguing for their position, should seek to fully understand those who disagree and help them think about the emerging direction from their vantage point. As Gardner puts it:

> The purpose of a mind-changing encounter is not to articulate your own point of view but rather to engage the psyche of the other person. In general, the more that one knows about the scripts and the strengths of the other person, the resistances and resonances, and the more that one can engage these fully, the more likely one

will be successful in bringing about the desired change—or at least holding open the possibility of such changes.[16]

Dialogue is the best way to discover these scripts, strengths, resistances, and resonances. These conversations may ultimately lead to broadening the emerging vision to embrace the ideas of these opinion leaders, accommodating their concerns, or simply opening the possibility that participants will have a better understanding of each other. These conversations reduce the likelihood that opinion leaders who disagree with the new direction will become part of the resistant. In the best of all worlds, such conversations may lead to these opinion leaders changing their minds. But if minds are not changed, these conversations identify concerns and contrary opinions that will be helpful to leaders in crafting the change message to make it most easily heard and appreciated by the near peers of the opinion leaders.

Even more fundamentally, all open-minded and respectful conversations demonstrate procedural fairness, the importance of which was outlined in chapter 3. Trust is the currency of leadership and the ground of hope, and procedural fairness helps maintain and even strengthen trust. When contrary-minded opinion leaders perceive that a direction-setting process has been fair, then they are more likely in the end to join the majority in pursuing the goal. Conversely, the perception of unfairness is one reason why those who once simply disagreed become part of the resistant. When opinion leaders demonstrate the values of participation (that all share control), inclusion (that all belong), respect (that everyone is valued), and affirmation (that what people find meaningful is considered important), they do their best to bring on board opinion leaders who disagree.

## Strategy 3: Focus Groups of Opinion Leaders

Focus groups that bring together opinion leaders who hold different opinions about the emerging direction are another effective strategy, both for fostering a diffusion network and for influencing the contrary minded. For example, we used focus groups before introducing contemporary elements into our traditional worship service. Each focus group included two segments of the congregation: longtime respected seniors who were opinion leaders and young adults who had grown up in the congregation, were well known to these seniors, and were opinion leaders in their own right. Many of these seniors had taught these younger adults as children in church school or worked with them in the youth programs, so the participants knew and appreciated each other. These mixed groups were asked to share their thoughts on some possible worship innovations. Through the discussion that followed, the seniors learned that these younger adults desired to see more contemporary elements added to worship, even though these younger adults grew up with the traditional service. The seniors heard the young parents' concerns that worship be appealing to their children. The seniors—mostly parents of grown children— could appreciate this desire. After all, the seniors wanted the same thing for their grown children and young grandchildren. The young adults, in turn, heard from the seniors about the meaning traditional worship held for them. These groups were not asked for decisions but only for their thoughts on contemporary worship. But what was more important, these opinion leaders left the focus groups with deeper understandings of each other and carried their new appreciation back to their own circles within the church. One participant—probably the most respected older adult in our congregation—afterward told me, "Certainly when I was their age I wanted to sing the kind of music I enjoyed then. We need to make room for them if we want our church to have a strong future." A thirty-year-old mother and lifelong member of our congregation told me after the discussion, "I understand that they enjoy the old hymns, and I wouldn't want to take that away from them." The diffusion network flowing from these focus groups moved our congregation toward a blended style of worship. It helped build intentions to accept the changes.

## Strengthening Capability and Context Beliefs

During dialogue, congregants reconsider their capability and context beliefs relative to the emerging vision. The emergence of a direction for the future will naturally prompt congregants to ask the question, Are we able to do it? Congregants need to believe that the goal is attainable through the congregation's own efforts and the congregation's context will enable it to attain the goal. If congregants have weak beliefs, then discussion during this step often stalls, losing its energy, clarity, and effectiveness. Stalled discussion is one of the best indicators that congregants' answer to the question, Are we able to do it? is no. The emerging vision may be appropriate, but congregants won't find it compelling if they don't believe they can attain it.

There are three ways to deal with weak capability and context beliefs. The first is to strengthen these beliefs, which is the most appropriate response when the congregation truly is able to attain the goal. Enactive and vicarious experiences in mastery as well as persuasion are effective means for strengthening these beliefs. These strategies are explored in chapter 3. Modifying the vision is the second approach. If the vision is changed so that people perceive it as more realistic, then capability and context beliefs will improve. The final approach is to break down the overall vision into a series of sequential objectives. What appears overwhelming as a whole may not be as daunting when people see it as a collection of more specific, realizable goals. This approach brings to mind an old joke. How do you eat an elephant? One bite at a time. Sometimes the vision needs to be portrayed in bite-sized pieces.

Leaders must not jump to the conclusion that congregants' weak capability and context beliefs are the consequence of congregants' inaccurate evaluations of their abilities. Sometimes weak beliefs are congregants' accurate assessment of the achievability of a proposed goal. Consequently, weak beliefs should always prompt leaders to reevaluate both the feasibility of the emerging vision as well as the congregation's beliefs about itself.

## Preparing for the Deliberation Step

As the dialogue step draws to the end, congregants are clear about the discrepancy gap and leaders understand the motives and attitudes associated with the gap. A goal or vision for the future has emerged (but may not yet be articulated with clarity), and leaders appreciate the motives and attitudes of congregants for and against the new direction. Moving on to deliberation depends on a positive answer to the question, If the congregation were asked today to affirm the emerging vision, would a good majority of the congregation approve it? Before leaving dialogue, leaders must be confident that a majority of congregants have already made the personal decision to accept—and even desire—change. Knowing that a majority favors the emerging direction assures leaders that they have a workable and acceptable vision, but what leaders might not yet have is the largest majority attainable. The goal of the deliberation step is to increase the size of the early majority so that a larger portion of the congregation feels motivated to pursue the vision.

Conversely, staying in dialogue provides the best opportunity to strengthen motivation to change if more work is needed. Until leaders know that a majority of the congregation is substantially behind the goal, they should continue with dialogue. Questions such as the following aid the assessment:

- What portion of the congregation appears to favor the emerging vision for the future?
- How might the vision be modified to increase the number of congregants who favor it? Should we pursue these modifications before moving on to deliberation?
- What can we do to increase the influence of the drivers and reduce the influence of the resisters? Conducting the force field analysis exercise is helpful at this point.
- Are there any prevalent attitudes that if changed would improve the acceptance of this vision? Are we able to influence a change in these attitudes?
- What side issues or conditions are we able to address so that more congregants will feel free to affirm the emerging vision?
- What are congregants' capability and context beliefs regarding this direction? Do congregants feel able or not able to attain this goal? Do we need to address weak capability and context beliefs before moving on to deliberation?
- What is the mood in the congregation? Is it positive or negative? Do congregants seem enthusiastic or wary about

the emerging direction? Are congregants focused on this direction or distracted by other issues in congregational life? Does the mood suggest we are able to move forward?

- How much urgency to proceed is there? Can we make time to address concerns raised by the questions above? If we don't have much time, what should our priorities be before moving to deliberation?

The answers to these questions may indicate a need to return to the discovery step. People who agreed with the need to change during discovery may not agree with the vision arising in dialogue. Put another way, attitudes not apparent during discovery may surface or form in response to the emerging direction. Leaders may have to loop back to discovery to influence change in these new emerging attitudes, and then revisit dialogue again before moving on to deliberation. As we saw earlier, the transtheoretical model suggests that spiraling through change (that is, taking one step back before taking two steps forward) is common and to be expected.

The dialogue step will likely take more time compared to the other four steps of the motivation-based change process. As the congregation moves into deliberation, leaders will know the majority of the congregation is behind the vision, and that knowledge will give confidence to the leaders as they continue the process. Taking the time to do dialogue well is an excellent investment in the congregation's future.

## CHAPTER 8

# Crafting and Sharing the Change Message: The Deliberation Step

*Persuasion is a symbolic process in which communicators try to convince other people to change their attitudes or behaviors regarding an issue through the transmission of a message in an atmosphere of free choice.*[1]
—*Richard M. Perloff*

The deliberation step moves congregants from the preparation stage to the action stage of the transtheoretical model. Intentions developed during dialogue are strengthened during deliberation. During this step, leaders widen acceptance and build momentum through the snowball effect, helping the rest of the early majority to choose the proposed direction and influencing late adopters to give the proposal serious consideration. The deliberation step ends when the congregation affirms a formal decision to adopt a goal.

Recall Senge's five different leadership approaches that move from minimum to maximum people involvement in developing a direction for the future. Dialogue is the step for testing, consulting, and cocreating a motivating goal and encouraging people to affirm the emerging direction. As congregants leave dialogue, the goal is pretty clear, and it is understood and accepted by many, but not all, congregants. The degree of acceptance of the goal at this point means leaders have less latitude to modify the goal, so testing, consulting, and cocreating must give way to selling. During deliberation leaders persuade people through a *change message*, which is a communication that sells the proposed direction to the congregation and prompts deliberation regarding the pros and cons of change.

Some people may be uncomfortable with the word *persuasion,* often because they believe the great myth that persuasion is about convincing people to do what they don't want to do. But the reality is this: people persuade themselves to change, based on information and arguments they consider. Persuasion is not about pushing choices but respecting choice makers and informing choice making. If a change message does not respect and inform people, then it will not persuade. Defined this way, persuasion is a fundamental role of leadership. Leaders propose new directions because they sincerely believe the congregation will be better off if a new direction is taken. Persuasion is about helping others appreciate what the leaders appreciate so that the congregation as a whole will agree to adopt a new direction.

Another misunderstanding of persuasion often leads to change messages that do nothing more than advocate the leaders' position from their perspective. Here the thoughts of Howard Gardner bear repeating:

> The purpose of a mind-changing encounter is not to articulate your own point of view but rather to engage the psyche of the other person. In general, the more that one knows about the scripts and the strengths of the other person, the resistances and resonances, and the more that one can engage these fully, the more likely one will be successful in bringing about the desired change—or at least holding open the possibility of such changes.[2]

In other words, a change message will be most persuasive if it reflects the attitudes of the recipients, appeals to their motives, acknowledges their concerns, meets their needs, and affirms their hopes.

This chapter is about how to craft such a change message. A change message is more than just one speech, since it will be shared formally and informally with different groups in a congregation whose members undoubtedly hold a variety of concerns and perspectives, requiring that the message be changed for different audiences. Repetition is also necessary, conveyed through sermons, brief announcements, printed materials, and discussions. But while the change message will be shared ultimately in diverse ways, crafting the message should be approached from the perspective that you will only have one occasion to address everyone to persuade them all to adopt a goal or vision. This perspective ensures that the essentials are covered in the change message and creates the starting point for variation. What follows are suggestions to consider when crafting the basic message.

## The Audience for the Change Message

Orient the change message to the unconvinced in order to increase the size of the early majority. A message that only advocates the leaders' position will tend to affirm those who already accept the goal. After all, the unconvinced, compared with the convinced, may

- have different motives and attitudes,
- see the proposed change as bringing different gains and losses,
- have different expressions of language, or
- emphasize different narratives of the congregation's past and present.

Asking the question, Who is the change message for? helps you determine whose psyche you wish to engage and is the first step in crafting a change message.

## Components of a Change Message

The design of an effective change message has been thoroughly studied over the past several decades. What follows comes from the work in organizational change of Auburn University business professors Achilles Armenakis and Stanley Harris and provides a simple, solid, five-component structure for selecting the content of a change message.[3]

## Component 1: The Discrepancy Gap

The discrepancy gap is the core component of a change message, describing the gap between the current situation and the proposed vision or goal as well as a broad outline of the plan to move from one to the other. In describing the current reality, note the real concerns about remaining with the status quo. Present concerns in a thoughtful, measured, and care-filled way from a middle-ground position—between sugarcoating concerns and a "The sky is falling!" rant. The proposed direction for the future should be clearly defined and easily understood, expressing hope and highlighting the unconvinceds' motives for pursuing the goal. Whether the direction is called a vision or a goal, the seven characteristics of a well-crafted goal (found in chapter 2) provide excellent criteria for formulating and articulating the direction. If there are any obstacles along the way to realizing the vision, then note them as well, along with plans for overcoming these obstacles.

In recent years in both the church and the business world, there has been a debate about whether change leaders should emphasize hopes or concerns. Both the "broaden and build" theory of Barbara Frederickson, psychologist at the University of North Carolina at Chapel Hill, and the popular appreciative inquiry process encourage leaders (in Johnny Mercer's phrase) to "accentuate the positive."[4] This group would have us avoid the motivational force of concerns. Yet others, such as Harvard's John Kotter and MIT's Edgar Schein, assert that people will not depart from the status quo unless they perceive some risk in remaining the same.[5] For them the change message must highlight negatives. The debate continues.

Some people have an ethical issue with emphasizing negative-sounding concerns in a change message, because they believe messages like this will foster fear and motivate coercively. People who believe this are correct to a degree, given that many change consultants and books suggest that leaders must paint the picture of a "burning platform" (that is, the status quo on which the organization stands is steadily being destroyed, putting everything at risk) in order to motivate action. Eliciting fear for its motivational power can be coercive and unethical if the approach is manipulative, making people believe they have little choice but to accept change. We should not dismiss, however, the authentic arousal of concern as a motivator. People often motivate by eliciting concern for appropriate reasons. Parents tell their children to be wary of strangers, because a stranger might hurt them. A doctor instructing a diabetic patient speaks frankly of the serious consequences of an improper diet. People are motivated to act when something they value is at risk of being lost.

I don't think anyone is critical of a positive emphasis on hope in a change message, although unethical appeals to hope also occur. Hope-centered change messages become coercive when they employ the bait and switch tactic, which promises a rosier consequence of change than will actually be realized (such as "Contemporizing our worship service will bring in new, young families in droves"). The unrealistic promise is the bait people swallow, but disappointment—and likely decreased motivation—will follow when people figure out that they have been duped. Being hopeful about what change will achieve is important for a change message, but honesty is the best policy.

Despite the debate, it is still quite apparent that people are most likely to change when they are motivated by both the push motives of concern and the pull motives of hopes. I side with those who believe, in general, that people will not change unless they have concerns about their current reality that motivate change. Certainly, concerns generate anxiety, but anxiousness is tempered by a realistic and confident hope that something can be done to address the concerns. Hope, then, not only pulls people forward into change but also harnesses and channels the motivation of concern. In this way the whole of the discrepancy gap will motivate people.

## Component 2: Appropriateness of the Proposed Change

The first component highlights *what* needs to be done to close the discrepancy gap. The second component explains *why* this specific goal is the best way to deal with the gap compared to other possible interventions. Helping people accept the appropriateness of the goal is critical to the success of the change message. This component is so critical that Armenakis and Harris state frankly, "If a change message cannot convince others of the appropriateness of the change, then efforts should be made to reconsider whether it really is appropriate."[6]

In the dialogue step leaders discover any reasons why congregants may not like this goal or why they might prefer an alternate direction. If such differences in opinion exist, then the change message must explain the rationale for the proposed goal and why it is preferred over other options. This point raises a question about approach: is it better to present a one-sided message (focusing only on the merits of the proposed goal) or a two-sided message (comparing and contrasting the proposed goal to alternatives)? Studies have generally shown that two-sided messages influence attitudes more than one-sided messages.[7] That being said, the two-sided message must refute the opposing argument and clearly demonstrate why the proposed goal is to be preferred. If the alternative is not discounted and the two goals are simply compared, then the two-sided message is made weak and actually becomes less influential than a one-sided message. Presenting a two-sided message also demonstrates procedural fairness, since the leaders openly acknowledge that other options exist. The openness, honesty, and demonstration of respect (in that the leadership obviously gave the alternative idea due consideration) encourage congregants to trust their leaders and trust that the proposed goal is indeed the best.

## Component 3: Affirmation of Capability and Context Beliefs

The message needs to affirm congregants' capability and context beliefs that they can attain the goal and close the discrepancy gap. The ground of hope is trust, so when congregants trust that their own abilities and context will help them succeed, then hope is strengthened. Capability and context beliefs rely on the evidence of past experiences in achieving goals, so the change message should remind people of that evidence, conveying the message, "As we did then, so we can do now." Stories of the congregation's past are the obvious choice for providing this evidence. Capability beliefs can also be strengthened by pointing out who will be involved in leading the initiative. If people perceive these leaders as capable, the congregation as a whole will feel more capable. More than anything else this component of the change message must instill confidence.

## Component 4: The Availability and Commitment of Resources

Capability beliefs are strengthened, in part, by the assurance that the resources required to attain the goal will be available to help turn vision into reality. When congregants can see that the right people will be given the right tools, funds, and time to do the job, then trust is strengthened, which again builds hope. Embarking on change is always an adventure into the unknown for a congregation. The uncertainty about what will happen in the transition from current reality to goal attainment creates a degree of anxiety. Helping congregants appreciate that the required resources will be there reduces the amount of uncertainty and builds confidence.

## Component 5: Be Hopeful, and Honest, about the Personal Impact

Ultimately, many congregants will want to know the bottom-line impact change will have on them personally. Armenakis and Harris state that explaining personal impact well is as critical as describing the appropriateness of the proposed change. The reality often is that change comes with costs and perceived disadvantages to some congregants, if not for all, and people prefer not to bear costs and accept disadvantages. Regardless of how noble the vision is, self-interest plays a bigger role in our motivation than any of us would like to admit.

The work of the earlier steps in the motivation-based change process can pay dividends at this point:

- Commitment to stewardship of the future brings a greater willingness to bear costs in the present for the sake of those who follow the current generation.
- Understanding the discrepancy gap brings an appreciation of what lies in store for the congregation if the status quo is maintained, which is a cost congregants need to weigh against the perceived costs of change.
- The work of fostering attitude change typically affects the priorities of people's motives, and thus potentially reduces people's priority for self-interest.

The dialogue step prepares leaders for crafting the change message, because during that step leaders learn what the perceived costs are. If leaders can ameliorate or compensate for the negative consequences of change, they should communicate this in the change message, which will make the proposal more acceptable. If the costs are unavoidable, then honesty is the best policy. But so is hopefulness. Some of those congregants who will bear the perceived cost of change will agree to pursue change because they believe in the greater good. They may also come to see that meaning can be found in attaining the goal, which can compensate for the losses to a degree.

Chapter 9 will provide more ideas for dealing with dissent.

## Other Considerations for Shaping and Sharing the Change Message

The five components above form the frame of a change message and ensure that the message will be influential. A number of smaller considerations can strengthen the change message even more.

### The Role of Stories in a Change Message

As we saw in the previous chapter, stories have motivational power because they align with our psychological wiring. Consequently, stories shared in a change message often touch our hearts more than facts and figures. For example, you could say that younger families are slowly drifting away from involvement in a faith community because they don't find congregational life meaningful. Or, in its place, you could tell the story of one such family. Stories seem to make things more real to us. *The Last Lecture,* by the late Carnegie Mellon computer science professor Randy Pausch on achieving your childhood dreams, is an excellent example of the use of stories in a change message. His talk contains simple, homespun wisdom, conveyed through a collection of personal stories, that has struck many people as profound, hopeful, and motivating. A number of versions of *The Last Lecture* are available on YouTube, and it is worth viewing to see the influential power of story.

Communicating a vision of the future through story makes the vision more real than an objective goal ever could. Instead of simply saying, "The goal is to add ten thousand square feet to our building," describe the congregational life that will be given birth within the new addition. Similarly, capability and context beliefs can be affirmed and strengthened through stories of how the congregation successfully attained goals in the past or overcame an obstacle presented by society. The capability beliefs derived from vicarious mastery always come through the stories of other congregations ("who were once just like us") that successfully pursued a similar goal. Stories are not simply illustrations or mental rest stops in the flow of rhetoric. Narrative vividly conveys ideas with deep meaning that leave a memorable and motivating impact on listeners.

Another thing to be mindful of is how congregants recall and retell their history. Think about your own life story. You can tell it through the themes of your family life, work, interests and hobbies, travels, faith, and so on. Perhaps you have one or two habitual ways of telling your story, but they are not the only ways. All these thematic approaches to your life story are true, but at any specific moment only one theme may be pertinent. Yet we always know there are many more ways, through thematic narrative, to describe ourselves.

So it is with congregations. Congregants may find it hard to embrace change if they believe they will no longer be who they are. Congregants may hear the proposed change as a critique of the past and thus also a critique of what they find meaningful in the present. Leaders may be able to address these issues by re-storying the congregation through a new, relevant, and honest theme. I've already shared the story of how our congregation embraced the idea of being missional when our story was reframed through the theme of our historic mission activity. When a vision for the future is tied thematically to congregational stories of the past, then the vision can be seen as a natural extension of the congregation's current identity and a natural evolution in congregational life.

## If You Can, Reduce Perceived Uncertainty and Risk

Risk taking is often required in change, and the perception of risk too frequently kills a proposed initiative. Motivation increases when both the perceived uncertainty of the future and the perceived risk of change decrease. Some of this natural uncertainty can be offset when the vision for the future is described in as plausible a way as possible. Sensible and realistic plans also decrease the feeling of risk. It is also offset if congregants can see a reasonable degree of continuity between the congregation's present storyline and the future storyline described in the vision. Increased continuity implies less risk. A positive tone to the change message strengthens trust in the leaders and thus also reduces the sense of risk. Finally, you can hold up examples of congregations already doing what is proposed for your congregation. In effect, the future has already arrived for them, and their success in attaining the same goal can reduce the sense of risk for your congregation.

## Convey the Congregation's Readiness for Change

A congregation that is ready for change is ready to take risks. The change message can strengthen capability beliefs by helping congregants recall what they have considered and achieved up to this point, perhaps by embracing a greater stewardship of the future or by reorganizing to make change happen more effectively. Use the readiness-for-change audit questionnaire found in chapter 5 to review the congregation. What aspects of the congregation's readiness will strengthen confidence in the face of risks?

## Keep Arguments Simple

Change messages often present some analysis to make the case for change. The arguments are typically presented in causal statements (for example, "Mainline churches are declining because society is becoming more secular"). Try not to use more than three causal statements in support of a point, since people are able to process only a limited amount of information. Provide too much information, and they may not remember enough of the change message for it to leave a lasting impression.[8] Change messages are also complicated by unnecessary divergences from the essential message, such as including unnecessary background details, discussing issues that are not pertinent to people, or just plain rambling. Keep in mind the KISS principle (which I define as "Keep it simple and straightforward") when crafting a change message.

## Present the Change Message in Diverse Ways

In 2007 Al Gore won both an Academy Award and a Nobel Peace Prize for his movie *An Inconvenient Truth* because of its effectiveness in generating support for the environmental movement. The film is a change message that motivates primarily by fostering concern. It is substantively a lecture, but the message is presented in many different ways throughout the film. You see Al Gore walking on a stage and talking, but the film also looks at times like a National Geographic documentary. It presents not only facts and statistics but also real-life stories. It shows charts and graphs as well as thought-provoking photographs. Particularly effective was Gore's use of pictures of glaciers showing their dramatic decrease in size over a few decades. He even used a few stunts, such as riding a scissor lift up along the side of a huge projection screen in the lecture hall, following the leading edge of an animated graph on the screen as it soared upward and left the screen—literally going off the chart—proceeding up the wall toward the ceiling of the large lecture hall. It was a humorous moment in the film—Al Gore riding a scissor lift!—but as he went up and up into the darkness far above the stage, trying to catch up to the leading edge of the line on a graph, Gore conveyed nonverbally the out-of-control reality of climate change. The diversity of methods used to convey one single message is a major reason why so many people found this film so compelling. People respond differently to different communication methods. In addition, a message is reinforced in the minds of recipients when they receive it in a number of ways. Don't just be a talking head.

## Use Language that Helps People Hear the Message

Psychologist E. Tory Higgins and his colleagues at Columbia University have demonstrated that people have one of two orientations that moderate motivation. Some people have a promotion focus, which orients them to look for possible gains and motivates them to attain benefits. Other people have a prevention focus, which orients them to look for potential losses and motivates them to minimize losses. These very different orientations affect not only motivated action but also how people hear a change message. Promotion-focused people will tune in to a message for change that outlines the benefits. Prevention-focused people, on the other hand, will tune in to a change message that shows how a proposed goal will rectify something that is at risk of being lost. Prevention-focused people more easily hear a change storyline that says, "The life of our congregation was in balance. . . . This balance has been thrown off by . . . Now such-and-such is at risk. . . . The proposed way forward will restore this balance that we desire." Every congregation will have both types of people, so both styles of explaining the discrepancy gap should be used.

## Express Realistic Confidence

Confident speech projects credibility, which in turn fosters trust. When speakers qualify and hedge, hesitate and equivocate, they convey a lack of confidence in the vision they are proposing, which will breed a lack of confidence in those who are listening. Leaders can, and should, be honest about the uncertainty of success or the significance of hurdles in implementation. But if their speech expresses realistic confidence in dealing with uncertainties and overcoming hurdles, people will have more confidence and optimism themselves.

## Be Clear on How Procedural Fairness Has Been and Will Be Practiced

Achieving unanimity regarding a new direction is not always possible. Consequently, efforts should always be made to ensure fairness in the process leading up to the decision to move forward, because fairness communicates to those who disagree that they are respected and their thoughts are important. It will demonstrate to them, and indeed everyone, that the leaders have acted with integrity and are worthy of congregational trust. Procedural fairness helps congregants who find themselves in the minority after a direction-setting decision is made, because they can at least be confident that their point of view was heard and considered with care. The more leaders anticipate that a proposed vision for the future could be divisive, the more procedural fairness needs to be highlighted as a part of the change message.

## Speak to the Heart

Cognition can affect our feelings, and our feelings can affect the conclusions of cognition. It is important, then, to speak to both. The suggestions given thus far help craft change messages so that they appeal to the head. Outlining how to appeal to the heart is not as easy, because it is less reasonable and more visceral. I believe speaking to the heart comes down to a combination of three kinds of appeals.

The first kind of appeal to the heart activates a basic emotion in people (such as compassion, anger, fear, or pleasure) that in turn prompts motivated behavior. An evolutionary view on emotions suggests each basic emotion evolved to motivate specific actions to attain specific goals: fear, to attain personal preservation; anger, to remove obstacles to attainment; sadness, to bring others to one's aid; compassion, to prompt care; guilt, to correct our behavior; happiness and joy, as a reward for goal attainment; and so on.[9] The following message from *An Inconvenient Truth* attempts to evoke motivated action by appealing to the basic emotion of fear.

> You see that pale, blue dot? That's us. Everything that has ever happened in all of human history has happened on that pixel. All the

triumphs and all the tragedies. All the wars and all the famines. All the major advances. It's our only home. And that is what is at stake: our ability to live on planet Earth, to have a future as a civilization. I believe this is a moral issue. It is your time to seize this issue. It is our time to rise again to secure our future.[10]

Gore's change message is a stimulus that we receive and process. An emotional reaction, which is very rapid, easily informs and biases our cognitive thoughts, skewing how we then appraise, interpret, and respond to the change message. This evaluation, in turn, often prompts action. Indeed, the goal of *An Inconvenient Truth* is to do just this: motivate people to become more environmentally responsible.

Appreciating how this mechanism works may cause us to reflect on the morality of such appeals, since we can easily imagine how it could be abused, but emotion-based appeals are appropriate in different situations. For example, as people of faith we see nothing wrong when an appeal is made to our sense of compassion to motivate us to help in disaster relief. There are also times when strong fear appeals are warranted ("The theater is burning!"). So this emotional mechanism for motivation is neither bad nor good—it just is. But because of the potential for abuse, leaders need to be judicious in its use.

The second kind of appeal to the heart affirms core beliefs we hold and inspires us to act on our beliefs. On April 20, 1964, Nelson Mandela gave his opening statement in his own defense in the trial that would send him to the notorious Robben Island Prison for twenty-seven years. The closing words of his statement spoke of his deep personal convictions and spoke to the same convictions in the hearts of many South Africans, inspiring them to continue the struggle for racial equality. These final words became known as Mandela's "I am prepared to die" speech.

During my lifetime, I have dedicated myself to this struggle of the African people. I have fought against white domination, and I have fought against black domination. I have cherished the ideal of a democratic and free society in which all persons live together in harmony and with equal opportunities. It is an ideal which I hope to live for and to achieve. But if needs be, it is an ideal for which I am prepared to die.[11]

Mandela was released from prison in 1990. Three years later, he shared the Nobel Peace Prize with South Africa's President F. W. de Klerk for their peaceful efforts to bring greater democracy to South Africa. A change message like Mandela's "I am prepared to die" speech motivates because it appeals to the beliefs, values, and priorities (which are all motives) that we already hold dear and causes us to strengthen our current attitudes (our evaluations of our motives), so we choose to act on those motives. These appeals motivate us to act on what is important to us.

The third kind of appeal to the heart encourages self-fulfillment. We all carry within ourselves a sense of our best self that we hope to live out in life. Some appeals to the heart call us to recognize this best self and then inspire us to act more concertedly on these qualities. In other words, these appeals motivate us to become more of who we are. Randy Pausch in *The Last Lecture* makes this kind of appeal, which is why it is so inspiring and motivating.

> I'm dying and I'm having fun. And I'm going to keep having fun every day; because there's no other way to play it. . . . Having fun for me is like a fish talking about the importance of water. I don't know how it is like not to have fun.[12]

Many of us aspire to have fun, and we would prefer our outlook to be fun seeking, even in the midst of life's difficulties. That Pausch could affirm this desire while knowing he had only months to live inspires listeners to strengthen the same attitude that dwells in all of us.

The choice of words in a change message can also influence the heart. Graphic language, in the sense that it evokes vivid images, can be very helpful in this regard. Words such as *freedom, grace, beauty, suffering,* and *compassion* carry a truckload of meaning that has the potential to inspire listeners.

## Tie This Story of Change to THE Story

Be explicit in relating the proposed direction to your faith, relevant scriptural stories, and the congregation's own stories of faith. Its faith story is an overarching story that the congregation will affirm as important and meaningful to them. Tying the story of change to the story of faith demonstrates that what is being proposed here and now can be seen as an act of faithfulness to God's enduring purposes, which will make the proposal more meaningful and motivating.

## Choose Respected People to Communicate the Message

Some influential books on congregational leadership recommend that the lead clergyperson be the official spokesperson for the change message. This suggestion makes a good deal of sense in large congregations because the lead clergyperson is probably the most visible congregational leader. But instead of basing the choice simply on a person's office, consider who might be the most credible spokesperson for this new initiative. The best spokespeople should have as many of the following characteristics as possible: trustworthiness (perceived as honest and forthright, and people find them comfortable), expertise in the area being discussed (which adds credibility to the change message), and goodwill (they are known for holding the well-being of the congregation in their heart). An excellent spokesperson is able, through his or her speech, to convey honesty, sincerity, empathy, and confidence. These qualities strengthen people's trust in the messenger and thus also in the message.

## Give the Change Message Trial Runs

The dialogue step will highlight motives, attitudes, arguments, stories, and so on that leaders will want to include in the change message, because the message crafters will believe these considerations will make a difference. The resulting message, however, will only reflect the leaders' best guess regarding what will be most persuasive. Leaders will find out how influential the message is by taking the initial version and trying it out on individuals and groups. Much can be learned from the reaction and feedback, which will help refine the message in turn. There is always room for improvement.

## Once You Have the Best Message, Improvise!

This chapter provides suggestions to help you craft one comprehensive motivating change message that is most appealing to the widest possible audience. But the reality is that every congregation is composed of a variety of people. Consequently, the change message will need to be tailored to different groups of listeners. Once you have crafted the best overall change message, feel free to improvise.

## Repeat the Message, and Then Repeat It Again

It is common wisdom that repetition helps reinforce a message, but repetition has a downside as well. For people who oppose a new initiative, repetition of the change message tends to strengthen their negative attitudes toward the vision. Repetition works best for people who start with either a positive view or a neutral view of the goal. But even for this group, repetition can lose its effectiveness because of a phenomenon marketers call "wear out."[13] A message wears out once repetition no longer brings benefits, and repetition after this point becomes tedious to people. So repetition can work for you and against you. Leaders need to monitor people's reactions to repetition of the change message to gauge the frequency and duration of repetition.

# The Limitations of the Change Message

Well-crafted change messages are highly influential, but their motivational effect has limits. People's motives and attitudes may be strongly held and impervious to the change message. People may disapprove of a proposed goal so strongly that even the most brilliant change message will have no effect. A well-crafted change message is critical to creating motivation for change, especially among the early majority, but leaders cannot expect it to be all things to all people.

President Barack Obama's first inaugural address is an excellent example of the limitations of a very well-crafted change message. On January 20, 2009, the United States was mired in a current reality that had every American concerned. The housing market crisis and economic recession that began to unfold during the presidential campaign in 2008 deepened rapidly into a financial crisis in the two months between the election and Inauguration Day. President Obama's inaugural address was a masterpiece as a change message. After the usual courtesies, the new president opened his change message with the following words:

> That we are in the midst of crisis is now well understood. Our nation is at war against a far-reaching network of violence and hatred. Our economy is badly weakened, a consequence of greed and irresponsibility on the part 'of some but also our collective failure to make hard choices and prepare the nation for a new age. Homes have been lost, jobs shed, businesses shuttered. Our health care is too costly, our schools fail too many, and each day brings further evidence that the ways we use energy strengthen our adversaries and threaten our planet. These are the indicators of crisis, subject to data and statistics. Less measurable, but no less profound, is a sapping of confidence across our land; a nagging fear that America's decline is inevitable, that the next generation must lower its sights.
>
> Today I say to you that the challenges we face are real, they are serious and they are many. They will not be met easily or in a short span of time. But know this America: They will be met.[14]

President Obama began his address with the current reality concerns and went on to describe the discrepancy gap, using all five components of a change message. The full address is worth study—either as written text or a video recording, which are both available on the Internet. But how much influence did this speech really have on the American people? Some heard in the address echoes of their own hopes. Others responded cautiously or critically, because to them the proposed directions were simply wrongheaded. America was just as polarized after the delivery of the inaugural address as the nation was before the address.

There are lessons here for communities of faith. The change message is indeed critical, but we cannot expect it to do all the work of motivating people. Odds are that a compelling vision, sold passionately, will not win everyone over, because, as Howard Gardner writes, "minds, of course, are hard to change." This truth reinforces the need to do well the work of the earlier steps. The work of creating greater readiness for change in the first step will influence people to be more open to new directions. Discovery will influence attitudes so that people are more agreeable to change. Dialogue will clarify what needs to change and build consensus for a proposed direction. The change message will be most effective when it builds on the successful work of the earlier steps.

## The Early Majority during Deliberation

The primary audience for the change message is congregants who will become part of the early majority during deliberation. During this step congregants are influenced by two things. The first is the change message itself. During dialogue, the early majority is influenced by a loose and dispersed collection of motives, attitudes, and possible goals. During deliberation this collection of influences is gathered together, sifted, refined, and articulated in a well-crafted change message so that the best influences will have the greatest impact. While dialogue is like holding a discussion in the midst of a shower of paper confetti, deliberation is like having a discussion while holding a block of wood. Both objects are composed of the same material, but one is more substantial. Some of the early majority will find the confetti sufficient to influence them, while others will need to have, hold, and inspect the wood block during deliberation. So, leaders need to encourage ongoing discussion during deliberation.

But the change message, compelling as it is, will not be persuasive on its own for the entire early majority, because some hearers will not trust completely what the message conveys. For this group the evidence that the message is trustworthy is provided by what psychologists call social proof. Social proof is a form of conformity. When people feel uncertain about what to do, some people will take their cue from those who are certain about what to do. The logic of social proof goes like this: "If all these people believe pursuing this goal is the right thing to do, then it must really be the right thing to do." Some congregants need this kind of evidence before they will join the early majority, and it can be provided in several ways. Trust is strengthened when a person whom the congregation might naturally assume would not be in favor of the vision publicly supports it. It is strengthened when leaders report that specific groups have considered and endorsed the vision. It is strengthened when a fund-raising event for a proposed project has a large turnout and is a financial success. When informal conversations about the vision are generally positive, then trust is strengthened. The point is that some people will need more than a compelling change message to help them get on board with a new direction. A congregational vote to proceed with a vision provides the most obvious social proof, but this evidence comes too late in the process. Any opportunities to provide social proof that the congregation is substantially behind the new vision before an official vote will increase the size of the early majority and strengthen their motivation to pursue the goal.

## The Late Adopters during Deliberation

Late adopters are more skeptical than the early majority, and so they need more time and evidence to be convinced of the merits of change. In my use of Rogers's term, late adopters represent those who will adopt the vision for the future after the formal decision to proceed is made. The initial portion of late adopters will join the early majority at the time the congregation ratifies the vision for the future. As stated above, a congregational vote to approve direction is a form of social proof that the adopted vision is the best one. The first late adopters are content to go with the flow in the direction most congregants appear to prefer.

Most late adopters, however, will come on board during the implementation phase of change as the vision is turned into reality. But that being said, they can be influenced in this earlier step by a change message that is crafted with their needs in mind. Late adopters are skeptical, in part, because of their fear of loss. Again, if there are ways to ameliorate or compensate for the negative consequences of change, then they can be noted in the change message. Also, many people tend to initially overestimate the impact of proposed change. Late adopters can be helped when leaders are very clear in component 5 of the change message about what is changing and what is not. Late adopters are also more risk adverse compared to the early majority, so explaining how people will be supported through the transition of change will help many feel more secure.

Finally, some skeptics may look for specific evidence during implementation that they need before they will be convinced to join the movement. For some it may be proof of the appropriateness of the direction and for others it may be proof that strong capability and context beliefs are warranted. Some skeptics will want to see with their own eyes that the personal impact is not as great as feared. The change message, then, could provide advance notice regarding when the needed evidence will emerge. For example, if late adopters are skeptical that the needed fifty people will actually volunteer to make the vision a reality, then the change message can indicate the target date for recruitment. While this information won't change the minds of late adopters during deliberation, it will give them some assurance that the evidence is forthcoming during deployment. Dealing with late adopters will be covered more fully in the last two chapters of the book.

## Moving toward the Moment of Decision

The lead pastor I worked with for nine years had a saying: "Don't ask the congregation to make a significant decision until people are ready to make it." If care is taken in the earlier steps, then leaders can be confident that a large majority is ready to ratify the vision. But conducting one final go, no-go assessment before asking the congregation to approve a direction is prudent. If the proposed direction is critical to the congregation's future, and the congregation votes it down, then the idea may be beyond resurrection in the future. The five components of a change message can be turned into questions for evaluating the congregation's specific readiness to make the proposed change:

- Do congregants appreciate the importance of this discrepancy gap and feel the need to deal with it?
- Do congregants understand and accept this proposed direction as the most appropriate one for us to pursue for dealing with the gap, and are they motivated to do so?
- Are our context and capability beliefs strong enough to help us pursue this vision for our future?
- Are congregants confident that we can provide the necessary resources for attaining this goal?
- Do congregants understand and accept the anticipated costs of change?

Conducting this kind of assessment prior to any final decision helps the leaders determine what outstanding motivational issues need to be addressed, how much time may be needed before the final decision is made, and even whether the vision still needs to be taken back, reviewed, reworked, and re-presented. The more critical a goal or vision is for a congregation's future, and the more significant the proposed change is for a congregation, then the more certain leaders will want to be that the most congregants possible are prepared to make a positive choice for change at the time the congregation is asked to ratify the vision.

The formal decision to adopt the goal or vision and proceed with implementation is the transition point between the deliberation step and the deployment step. At this point leaders may assume that the motivational work is done, because the majority has decided to proceed and dissenters will never have their minds changed. This perspective misses two important points. First, deployment is a time to influence both late adopters and the resistant to join the movement for change. Second, the motivation of the majority must be maintained during the implementation phase as people engage in the hard work of effecting change. This means that everything that has been accomplished to this point will need to be reiterated and reinforced moving forward. These two concerns will be covered in the last two chapters.

# Dealing with Dissent: Rethinking Resistance to Change

*A curious and troubling aspect of human nature is that reasonable men and women often resist acting on social knowledge that would advance their collective self-interest.*[1]
—James O'Toole

The idea that congregations resist change is so commonplace that it has become a cliché. The statistics indicating the prevalence of congregational conflicts make one wonder about how many people have adopted for themselves the 1960s slogan for Tareyton cigarettes: "I'd rather fight that switch." I have seen a few clergy come through change initiatives sufficiently battered that they adopted personal "never again" policies. I have also seen clergy so demoralized by the apparent need for congregational change on one hand and congregational intransigence on the other that they simply resigned. They chose to switch, rather than fight.

This chapter explores resistance to change. Diffusion theory suggests that opponents to change can be divided into two groups: the late adopters and the resistant. Late adopters are skeptical but still potentially open to change if they are given the right evidence in favor of change. The resistant, by comparison, oppose the proposed change. The culture of the congregation, the issue at hand, and what congregants perceive as the personal cost of change may spawn resistance among any number of congregants, and the group may be weak or powerful in its force. Congregants may become resistant at any point in a change process. Some people may begin to oppose new directions during discovery, because they don't want the status quo to change. Other people may become resistant during dialogue, because they don't like the tentative direction that emerges. Still others may shift from the late adopter category to the resistant during deliberation, because their position hardens during debate. Leaders may not be able to distinguish clearly between the late adopters and the resistant, but the distinction needs to be maintained, because the groups have very different needs. While the resistant, by definition, may never accept the new direction, the fact that Everett Rogers's diffusion theory calls this group laggards suggests the possibility that they might in time.

The nineteenth-century philosopher John Stuart Mill called resistance "the despotism of custom,"[2] but does resistance have to be viewed that way? A growing number of people in organization development have been asking this question over the past twenty years. For them, resistance to change is often viewed as the consequence of inadequate leadership skill, of an imposed change, of making the well-being of the community secondary to an issue, of a failure to involve people in formulating goals and plans, and even of what is simply a bad idea. When managers and leaders view resistance as an opportunity for collaboration rather than conflict, then the concerns of the resistant may become important insights that can actually add value to an important change initiative.

Many leaders view resistance as an anchor that results in organizational immobility. But what if we think of resistance as a rudder that can help steer a congregation toward change? This reimaging of resistance is important, because it builds on the reality that our culture is one of choice. When people suspect their autonomy and power to choose are at risk, they will begin to resist and push back against change.

## Diagnosing the Roots of Resistance

Diagnosing the root cause of resistance is not always easy. Some people may silently bear a grudge that will never be voiced. The reasons given by others may actually be smokescreens that do not reflect people's true concerns. Others may tell you their problems with a proposal, but not reveal the depths of their unhappiness. Others may publicly continue to show signs of support but speak or work against the proposal behind the scenes. In addition, resistance may emerge at any time as people pass through the transtheoretical model's stages of change. Below is a list of seven diagnostic questions for determining the source of resistance. The first two questions deal with trust issues, and the following questions use the five components of the change message as a diagnostic scheme.

## Do People Trust Their Leaders?

Trust is the currency of leadership that is slowly earned and quickly lost. The question, Do people trust their leaders? is the first one leaders must ask themselves if they face resistance, because concerns are hard to address if some congregants do not trust the leadership. Leaders need to ask themselves, Do the resistant believe we have their best interests at heart? Do they believe we can act wisely? Do they believe we are dependable? The resistant may become cautious and untrusting of their leaders if the resistant believe that the proposed direction is more important to the leaders than concern for the resistant. Strengthening trust, then, depends on showing people that they are as important, if not more so, than the goals.

Here is a list of simple steps for leaders to take to foster trust:

- Be inclusive of the resistant by providing opportunities for them to express freely their concerns and feelings. People who find themselves in the minority during congregational change often worry that they will be forgotten in the process, which may strengthen their resistance.
- Be open to alternative courses of action that the resistant may be able to accept. Give priority to finding win-win solutions during discussions.
- Promise to give serious consideration to good suggestions, and then do what has been promised. But never promise more than you are able to deliver, because being undependable erodes trust.

- Act out of integrity and empathy rather than expediency. Considerate behavior demonstrates that people are more important than the process.
- Maintain ongoing, open communication with the resistant. Consistent and conscientious communication demonstrates respect and care.
- Take responsibility publicly for any mistakes made in the process of conceiving, developing, and adopting the vision. Contrition goes a long way to recoup lost trust.
- Report back publicly about the concerns of the resistant and where their ideas have, or haven't, been incorporated in the proposals. Give credit where credit is due. Demonstrate respect for the resistant by explaining with care which aspects of their concerns could not be addressed, and why.

Taking these kinds of actions is an expression of both pastoral care and leadership. In response, the resistant will, one hopes, feel that they have been taken seriously as participants in the change process.

## Do People Believe that the Visioning and Planning Process Has Been Fair?

The second question, Do people believe that the visioning and planning process has been fair? also focuses on trust but more specifically on procedural fairness. Resistance increases when people believe that the process of conceiving and adopting a vision has not been fair. Leeds School of Business professor Russell Cropanzano and his colleagues believe people will perceive a situation as unjust and respond with resistance if one or more of four needs have not been met.[3] These four needs, in turn, suggest four values for leaders to keep in mind when designing a process for determining congregational direction:

- *The need for control.* Resistance can arise if people believe that they have not played a sufficient role in determining their own future. The value that recognizes this need is *participation.*

- *The need for belonging.* Some congregants may feel alienated from the majority of the congregation by the decision-making process, prompting greater resistance. The value that recognizes this need is *inclusion.*
- *The need for self-regard.* The belief that one has been unjustly treated may have a negative impact on one's sense of dignity, self-respect, and self-worth. An unfavorable outcome may lead one to assume, "Those people don't think I am important." The value that recognizes this need is *mutual respect.*
- *The need for meaning.* Sometimes people reject a change process because they think, "This is not how a congregation is to behave." For these people, the change process challenges something meaningful in their understanding of congregational identity and may lead to accusations of hypocrisy or even produce a crisis of personal faith. The value that recognizes this need is *affirmation.*

I wish the need to treat people with respect and fairness was so obvious that it didn't require treatment in a book on motivation, especially for congregations. Yet congregational conflict, which we have seen is quite prevalent, often has its origins in people's perceptions of insufficient procedural fairness in a change process. Such conflicts can be avoided if we enact the simple fairness formula from Jesus: "In everything do to others as you would have them do to you; for this is the law and the prophets" (Matt. 7:12). Procedural fairness also helps the contrary-minded accept the final chosen direction. Cropanzano and his colleagues have shown that people are generally able to accept outcomes that are not their preference if they believe the vision creation process was fair and they felt respected and accepted throughout the process.

## Does Resistance Arise from a Lack of Understanding?

Leaders need to determine whether people understand why the change is being proposed. Has resistance arisen because some people do not understand fully the discrepancy gap, the proposed goal, or the rationale for the goal? If the answer is yes, then a better understanding may result in different attitudes toward the initiative.

Reengaging the resistant using the discovery step is the appropriate response to this kind of resistance, taking an information-based approach that encourages people to consider the facts of the matter. Studies have shown that the most effective means of encouraging attitudinal change is by helping people update their understanding of a situation.[4] Ask the resistant why they believe the proposed direction should not be adopted, and in their answers look for inaccuracies in the facts that form the basis of their attitudes. Providing people with a different and better factual basis for their understanding often prompts reassessments and new attitudes.

### Does Resistance Arise from People's Evaluation that the Proposed Goal Is Not Appropriate?

Resistance about the appropriateness of the proposed goal is where people's beliefs and values come into play most strongly. People may think singing contemporary praise songs is not appropriate for a traditional congregation or spending money on staff is not appropriate for a mission-minded congregation. Some congregants may prefer that the piano stay where it is currently located because it just looks better there, even though the choir can't hear it!

The response in this situation also involves reengaging the resistant using the discovery step. Asking the resistant why they think the goal is inappropriate helps leaders discover the beliefs and values at the heart of the resistant's attitudes. Attitude change depends on the resistant changing the relative priority of their current beliefs and values compared to other beliefs and values they hold.

### Does the Resistance Arise from the Perceived Impact of the Proposed Goal?

The strongest resistance comes from people who perceive that the proposed change will have a negative impact on them, and the greater the perceived impact, the greater the resistance will be. The hedonic principle is a strong motivator for people when faced with a negative impact: people prefer what gives them pleasure and avoid what they find displeasing.

The response in this situation is to help the resistant see their preferences in a new light. People will probably have a complex mix of preferences, motives, and attitudes about a proposed change for their congregation. How current reality and the benefits of change are framed and articulated may prompt people to change their priorities within that mix. Leaders may also be able to assist the resistant to appreciate how they themselves could benefit in some way from the proposed change, in either the short term or the long term. For example, some congregants may not like the idea of increasing their giving so their congregation can afford to add a staff position for youth ministry because that staff person will directly benefit only the youth. But the resistant in this case might benefit, because the pastor will no longer lead the youth program and subsequently will have more time to be with older members. Addressing the concerns of congregants on occasion requires an appeal to their self-interest.

But appeals to wider interests beyond the self also work with some people. We all harbor in our thoughts a sense of our best self and prefer our actions align with it. Consequently, we struggle at times when there is a misalignment, and the resulting cognitive dissonance motivates us to find realignment, either by bringing our actions in line with our best selves or by adopting a new sense of self that aligns with what we want to do. When self-interest is driving resistance, leaders may remind congregants to consider the values of their best selves.

Social anthropologist and business professor James O'Toole has written that leaders must convince people of "the rectitude," or the moral virtue, of the proposed change.[5] This reminding takes place when leaders encourage congregants to live out values such as inclusivity, cooperation, mutual respect, pursuing mutual interest, generosity, compassion, and fairness. Strengthening a congregation's stewardship of the future also encourages people to appreciate interests beyond their own. This approach works with some people because it appeals to a different kind of self-interest: our preference to portray ourselves in the best light possible, with our actions aligning with our sense of our best self.

But even people who agree with a proposal may resist because they want to avoid the instability inherent in the transition period of change, which creates a different kind of impact. Any person or organization facing change is going somewhere they have never been before, which prompts questions and worries about whether the goal can be achieved. In addition, the transition period between the current reality and attaining the goal is often turbulent, because the congregation is no longer fully what it was but not yet what it aspires to be. For some people, the fear of instability in the transition period is enough to make them want to avoid change. These congregants require a greater sense of security, which comes from confidence that the goal is attainable, trust in the leaders who are implementing plans, assurance that the resources will be available and the anticipated costs will be the only costs, and so on. This group will also need to be assured that the leadership and congregation generally will support them through the transition of the implementation period.

## Does the Resistance Arise from People's Belief that the Goal Is Unattainable?

Resistance due to people's beliefs that the goal in not attainable focuses on people's capability and context beliefs. If people speak directly about their weak beliefs, then leaders can use some of the strategies found in chapter 3 for strengthening context and capability beliefs. Congregants may hesitate to express verbally, however, their belief that the congregation is incapable of achieving success, because doing so could make them feel self-conscious or embarrassed. These congregants might also fear the reaction of others who do not share their opinion or may wish to avoid hurting the feelings of those who believe in the congregation's capability. Consequently, these congregants may express their opinion nonverbally through a common form of resistance: avoidance.

If congregational discussion about a proposal fades away or people shift their focus to other endeavors, then wise leaders should suspect that the reason is weak capability and context beliefs. Delicate inquiry about the change in congregational behavior and its reasons can bring these weak beliefs to light. Getting the true answer, though, often takes patience and persistence, and when the answer is discovered, people need to be handled with care.

## Does the Resistance Arise from People's Belief that the Resources Aren't Sufficient to Accomplish the Goal?

People will hesitate to commit time and effort toward a goal if they don't think the nuts and bolts they need to attain the goal will be there. Factors may be the timeline, finances, staff support, the number of capable people needed, outside expertise, specific technical help (for example, people who have the expertise to create a website or a database), and so on. These concerns are addressed by providing as much evidence as possible that the resources will be there. On the other hand, if the resistant have identified an actual weakness in the plan, then addressing resource shortcomings will reduce resistance.

It is not unusual for resistance to persist even after the leaders have done their level-headed and empathetic best to address the concerns of the resistant. Persistent resistance probably indicates that these congregants simply do not like what the change will mean for them. So if resistance persists, leaders should go back to the earlier diagnostic question, Does the resistance arise from the perceived impact of the proposed goal? Perhaps the only way to address the concerns of the resistant is to adjust the vision for the future.

## Talking with the Resistant

People who disagree with a proposed direction often expect that they need to resist in order to have an impact on decision making, and so they approach discussion mentally prepared to debate the issue and defend their interests. For some people, getting ready to resist is like girding for battle. Leaders dampen this behavior by rolling with the resistance, accepting it as a necessary phase in significant congregational change, demonstrating an openness and sympathy for their concerns, and then giving their issues serious consideration. By seeking to understand the resistant and their issues without criticizing, judging, or blaming, leaders demonstrate respect. Resistance is often used as a tactic to exert strong influence. A respectful and accepting attitude—on the part of the leaders as well as the congregation as a whole—disarms this tactic and opens the possibility for real conversation, rather than conflict.

Through conversation with the resistant, leaders hope to discover whether the source of the resistance is attitudes or motives. An attitude is an evaluation of a belief, such as, "The congregation's future is not in jeopardy," "Presbyterians do not do evangelism," or "The culture of our society has not changed significantly over the past forty years." If resistance is rooted in attitudes, then helping people reconsider their beliefs may lead to different attitudes and consequently reduced resistance. If resistance is rooted in motives, then helping people reconsider and change the priority among their pertinent motives may reduce resistance.

What leaders want to avoid is causing attitudes to become more entrenched. As we saw in chapter 2, debating a proposal can cause people to defend their attitudes, which means they may not actually hear, reflect on, and appreciate the merits of a different point of view. In addition, the act of defending attitudes tends to make attitudes more rigid and less amenable to change. If positions become rigid, then a process for conflict resolution may ultimately be required. Effort given to avoid confrontation is invaluable.

Any of the discussion methods mentioned in this book may be of use to leaders for engaging the resistant. In particular, the three strategies outlined in chapter 7 for engaging traditional opinion leaders can be very helpful: one-on-one discussion using a format from motivational interviewing, holding a meeting of the resistant and leaders, or focus groups. The World Café method for group discussion may also be helpful. "Open house" drop-in gatherings provide forums for people to ask questions for clarification, give their opinion, or simply listen to the thoughts of others. What follows are two other methods for facilitating discussion in the congregation between proponents of the new direction and the resistant.

## Fishbowl Discussion

The fishbowl exercise is a panel discussion for an audience. It is not a decision-making strategy but an educational event. The exercise usually involves five to eight people (the "fish") who are seated in a circle and hold a conversation in full view of a larger group of listeners, who are seated in a surrounding circle (the "fishbowl"). One member of the panel should be a moderator, who will facilitate the progress of the discussion. If the event involves a large number of people, then several fishbowls can take place concurrently. Typically, one panelist chair is left empty at the beginning of the exercise so that members of the audience may join the panel and participate for a short while as visitors. This is a very good method for discussing the concerns about a proposed goal, because it provides a great deal of transparency. The goal of this exercise is not to reach a consensus on direction but rather to help everyone—on the panel and in the audience—understand the issues and concerns as well as the divergent attitudes and motives held by congregants.

I recommend that panel members be handpicked for the event to ensure that the different opinion groups in the congregation are represented. People should also be chosen based on their ability to participate in an articulate and respectful way. If the panelists are able to display these qualities in discussion, they will encourage the expression of the same qualities among the audience. The exercise may be concluded with an open-mike opportunity for members of the audience to share what they have learned through the discussion and perhaps how their own opinions have been changed or reinforced.

## If-Then Exercise

The if-then exercise helps participants analyze a proposal for change and potentially grow in their understanding of what other people think about the proposal, perhaps even coming to better appreciate their own position. For this exercise to work the group must unanimously agree that the discrepancy gap is real and that its issues must be addressed. This starting place becomes the statement of need that the exercise will address. Like the fishbowl exercise, the if-then exercise is not a decision-making strategy but an educational one.

Gather participants into small discussion groups of six to eight members, mixing people who hold different opinions. The exercise facilitator begins by affirming the people's common concern for the discrepancy gap and participants' common commitment to the congregation, which motivates them to deal with the gap. Participants are then given personal time to sketch a simple outline of their thoughts using the following formula: "*If* we do ____ (state a proposal for change), *then* ____ (describe the desired outcome), *because* ____ (provide a simple rationale for the idea)." For example, if the issue is membership decline in a congregation, then a participant might write: "*If* we adopt a contemporary style of worship, *then* we will experience membership growth, *because* young people prefer this worship style." Participants may list as many ideas as they wish to explain "*because*."

After the individual work is completed, participants, one at a time, present their personal if-then statements to the others in their discussion group. After each person has presented, group members are encouraged to ask questions for clarification. Group members are not to evaluate or critique the proposal. Seeking clarification is a process much like peeling an onion and can eventually reveal inner layers—the beliefs, assumptions, values, priorities, attitudes, and motives of the one explaining the proposal. This first part of the exercise may take about ninety minutes, including introductory remarks and directions by the facilitator.

Once all the if-then statements have been presented, the work shifts to consolidate the individual ideas. Provide a few stations around the room that are identified by a pair of flipchart pages hung side by side on the wall. Leave sufficient room between the stations so that people can gather around them comfortably. The facilitator at this point asks someone to read his or her if-then statement and, once it is read, asks whether any other people have a similar statement. These people are assigned one station and directed to post their if-then statements around the two sheets of flipchart paper. Next, the group agrees to a common if-then statement, which they post as the proposal for their station. The facilitator continues to seek out new groups with similar statements and directs them to work at other stations. As each group finishes developing its if-then statement, participants return to their chairs. Then the facilitator provides a brief lesson in how to conduct a force field analysis exercise, explained in chapter 6. This portion of the exercise will take up to forty-five minutes to complete.

During a break at this point, the facilitator encourages participants to wander around the room, with snack and beverage in hand, and to look at what is posted at the different stations. Participants are then directed to choose a station at which to work for the next part of the exercise. There is one restriction: participants cannot choose the station where their own if-then statement is posted. The goal of this part of the exercise is to prepare to present this proposal—which is not their own—to all the participants. Groups conduct a round of force field analysis, using the two sheets to list driver and resister motives. The individual if-then postings at the station provide the initial resource for the force field analysis exercise, but encourage participants to go with the spirit of the exercise and add their own thoughts as well. Encourage them to conduct their work with respect for the people who believe this proposal is the best proposal.

Provide about thirty minutes for this work. Once this analysis is completed, each group presents the proposal at their station, highlighting the basic if-then statement, the most important elements of the rationale for the proposal, and the drivers and resisters for the proposal. People who originally posted at that station are then invited to make suggestions to improve the work. Once all the proposals are presented, the facilitator asks whether everyone is satisfied that his or her own idea has been fully considered. This portion of the exercise may take about one hour, or even more, depending on the number of proposals.

At this point the facilitator may look for emerging consensus. The facilitator asks if the exercise has caused any people to reconsider their own proposal, since the discussion of drivers and resisters may influence some participants to change their minds. Some participants may acknowledge that they now prefer a different option over their original one. If this is the case, poll everyone who posted to the proposal in question for permission to drop it from consideration. If agreement is not unanimous, then the proposal is kept for consideration. The remaining proposals, with all the associated materials, are referred to the leaders.

This exercise is not designed primarily for consensus building. Rather, it is intended to help individuals analyze their own thinking and better understand the thinking of other people in a collegial, cooperative setting. At the end of the exercise, the leaders will, at a minimum, better appreciate the reasons for resistance, which will be contained in the lists of drivers and resisters. The improved understanding, in turn, may lead to insights for accommodating the concerns of the resistant or ameliorating their loss. The product of the exercise will also help the leaders strengthen the change message.[6]

## Making Adjustments for the Resistant

Leaders have little choice but to respond to the resistant in some way. The treatment of the resistant has several potential consequences in a congregation engaging in change. The response may make the difference in whether the resistant feel alienated from the congregation. It may strengthen or weaken congregants' trust of their leaders. The response to the resistant often has a significant impact on the decisions of the late adopters. Finally, if not handled well, it may lead to ongoing conflict. How much adjustment the vision undergoes for the sake of the resistant depends on numerous factors, such as the strength of their motivation, the rigidity of their attitudes, the legitimacy of their concerns, the number of resistant congregants, the potential for chronic divisive behavior, the flexibility of the vision, and so on. The best possible direction for a congregation's future is not only the most necessary and practical one but also the direction the greatest number of congregants will embrace. Accommodating the resistant in some way may be necessary to create a vision for the future with the widest possible appeal.

The most straightforward response is simply to improve the change message. This modest adjustment is appropriate if the vision for the future is actually pretty acceptable to the resistant, but they have not appreciated how acceptable the vision really is. Leaders will assume that the message as originally crafted described the discrepancy clearly, presented the rationale cogently, showed the appropriateness simply, boosted capability and context beliefs, and satisfied concerns regarding the personal impact of the goal. But as the old saying goes, "If you really want to understand your church, try changing it." The change message often elicits comments and concerns leaders could not have foreseen, which often come most substantially from the resistant. This feedback will help leaders re-tailor the change message in a way more easily understood by the resistant and that addresses their issues directly.

Simply changing the change message, however, may not be enough. Adjusting the vision to some degree may also be necessary. In the long run, accommodating the concerns of the resistant may reduce resistance and increase the number of congregants affirming the vision. Accommodating the resistant will also demonstrate that the leaders are trustworthy, caring, and willing to be fair by exhibiting procedural justice. If the vision is changed, then elements that are left out at this stage could be adopted in a later phase of development.

But some goals cannot accommodate much change and still effectively address the underlying discrepancy gap. The all-or-nothing nature of some goals is worrisome to the resistant and a challenge for the leaders. In such situations, however, it may be possible to meet the concerns of the resistant in other ways. One approach is to ameliorate the impact of change on the resistant by making the new situation more tolerable for them. For example, imagine a congregation that wants to adopt a contemporary worship style. One option would be to have two worship services, each with its own distinct style—contemporary and traditional. This accommodation would not be a capitulation to the resistant but really amelioration.

Another approach is to compensate the resistant in some way for the loss they will experience in a congregational change. For example, if a Vietnamese-language congregation must be amalgamated into a neighboring English-language congregation due to financial realities, then the new combined congregation may provide a Vietnamese-language service once per month. This adjustment is certainly not the same as offering a weekly service and nurturing congregational life in the Vietnamese language, but the monthly service demonstrates the congregation's concern for their new members and a desire to support them.

## Transition

Everyone experiences loss during organizational change, which is never impersonal since people have some degree of connection to practices being left behind. While everyone feels loss to some degree, the resistant feel it most acutely. The work of management consultant

William Bridges helps leaders understand the needs of people experiencing what he calls transitions.[7] For Bridges, transitions

- begin with an ending, during which people let go of their old practices and identity;
- end with a new beginning, during which the new practices foster new purpose, identity, and energy; and
- have a neutral zone in between the ending and beginning, during which the unsettledness helps people adjust to new ways of acting and understanding.[8]

Bridges goes on to say that "the single biggest reason organizational changes fail is that no one has thought about endings or planned to manage their impact on people."[9] Transitions need to be taken seriously, especially if the leaders wish to support the resistant in the short term and hope to encourage some degree of acceptance of the change in the long term. Bridges's book *Managing Transitions* is an important resource for all leaders of faith communities in this era of congregational change. Bridges's approach can help leaders be attentive during dialogue and deliberation by listening for the potential experiences of loss that could come as a consequence of change, adjust the vision and its impact to minimize people's sense of loss (if possible), craft the change message, and plan support for those experiencing loss most acutely. Bridges offers ten recommendations to help people deal with loss during transition.

1. Identify Who's Losing What.[10] Who will feel the impact of the proposed change? What do they think they are losing? Look for possible chain reactions: what secondary changes may occur as a consequence of the planned change, and who will those changes affect? Think about the congregation as a whole, as well as its constituent groups and individuals.
2. Accept the Reality and Importance of the Subjective Losses.[11] Change that seems remarkably sensible and simple to leaders may appear dramatic and unwarranted to some congregants. The experience of loss is unique to each of us, and some people may react quite strongly to the proposed change. In some instances, congregants may be reacting out of their

previous experiences with change. The reaction of still others may stem from a fear that this change is only the first of more changes to come. Overreactions, when they occur, may point toward what some congregants feel they are actually losing.

3. Acknowledge the Losses Openly and Sympathetically.[12] Express simply, honestly, and directly what is actually being lost, as well as compassion for congregants who are experiencing the loss. By acknowledging people's feelings of loss in a time of change, leaders demonstrate that these congregants are important. Leaders may be tempted to soften the blow of change by minimizing its impact. This can unintentionally become a bait and switch tactic, however, with people discovering later on that the impact was greater than initially explained. The consequent feeling of being duped can result in even stronger negative reactions down the road, reduce congregational trust in its leaders, and put the vision in jeopardy. "Honesty is the best policy" from the very beginning.

4. Expect and Accept Signs of Grieving.[13] Expect to see classic reactions to loss, such as denial, anger, bargaining, anxiety, sadness, disorientation, withdrawal, and aimlessness. Anticipate these and respond pastorally to them. Congregants will not uniformly share the same feelings or experience their sense of loss with the same emotional intensity. In any large group such as a congregation, leaders should anticipate that the experience of grief among individuals will be quite varied.

5. Compensate for the Losses.[14] Bridges provides a helpful question to uncover potential ways to compensate for losses: "What might we give back to balance what has been taken away?" The response was covered above. Ultimately, it is unlikely that anything a congregation does will completely compensate for a loss. The hole may be filled somewhat, however, by providing something in place of what was lost.

6. Give People Information Again and Again.[15] Delaying communication of "bad news" to avoid hurting people's feelings is a natural response in times of loss, but it often leads to greater anger and mistrust. Acknowledging the potential or inevitability of loss from the beginning helps people adjust

to loss. Bridges also states that "threatening information is absorbed very slowly."[16] Calculate how much communication you think is necessary, then multiply that by three. Avoid half-truths and incomplete answers, for they will only lead to decline in trust in the end.

7. Define What's Over and What Isn't.[17] Clarifying what is changing reduces anxiety by limiting what congregants will worry about. If the messaging isn't clear about what is changing, people will make assumptions about the scope of change and potentially become more upset than need be. Lack of clarity may result in congregants continuing practices that leaders intend to end while also adopting the new practices. In addition, congregants may make unplanned—and unhelpful—changes.

8. Mark the Endings.[18] Formally acknowledge an ending during a designated worship service to help people come to closure on the past. Depending on the situation, creating a historical record or permanent public recognition of what was lost affirms that it was important to people and so must be remembered.

9. Always Treat the Past with Respect.[19] The past is never gone; it is always retained in our memory and our history. If the past is not treated with respect, then people may interpret this behavior as a lack of respect for them as people. Ask the question, How will we remember and honor the past? As I noted earlier, if the story of congregational change can be told as a natural extension of the congregation's story, then congregants will be more likely to believe their heritage is being respected.

10. Show How Endings Ensure the Continuity of What Really Matters.[20] Most endings in organizational change ensure the continuity of purposes and values that have higher priority than what is being given up. Remind the resistant that change will help preserve and strengthen aspects of the congregation that are also important to them. Individuals will often have several different and conflicting attitudes toward a proposed

change. Reminding people about what really matters helps them shift their focus from the attitudes that generate the feelings of loss toward attitudes that promote acceptance.

## One Final Possibility: A Humble and Gracious Retreat

Earlier I noted four adjustments leaders may make in response to the resistant, but there is also a fifth: don't proceed with the proposed vision. This final response might be an anathema to leaders, but it should not be viewed this way. The actual worst-case scenario for a congregation is rejecting an important proposal that then has no possibility of resurrection. Not proceeding with a proposal is a demoralizing experience for leaders, but putting the congregation's future in real jeopardy is even more serious. As Demosthenes wrote in 338 BCE, "The man who runs away may fight again."[21] The transtheoretical model reminds us that attaining a vision for the future may require more than one attempt at change, much like the experience of people who wish to lose weight or cease smoking. Prudence may prompt leaders to put a vision for the future on hold until the conditions for it ripen more.

Another form of retreat is to reduce the scale of the vision. Leaders manage change by controlling its scope and pace. Scope has to do with how much change to introduce at a time. Pace has to do with how fast to implement change. Substantial resistance may indicate that what leaders believe must happen requires smaller steps (a more limited scope) or a longer time frame (a slower pace). Limitations may make the vision more agreeable to the resistant now and keep the door open for other aspects to be reconsidered later.

## Always Maintain Hope for the Resistant

The resistant are least likely to join the movement for congregational change, but this does not mean leaders can simply write them off as a lost cause. Recall that Rogers calls the resistant *laggards*, which suggests they may change their mind in time, however slim that possibility may be. Leaders, then, must always be hopeful for the resistant. After all, some may surprise you.

During our building program, one congregant was a vociferous and very public opponent of the project. Yet on opening day he could be seen proudly giving tours of the new facilities to visitors from our neighborhood. That was a big surprise! While I pegged him as resistant for months, it turned out he was just a very late adopter. He was a retired chartered accountant with a fiscally conservative orientation. It turned out that he simply didn't believe we could build our addition and stay on budget, and so he expressed his ongoing opposition throughout the construction period. As soon as he learned the project was completed on budget, he became content with the project. This story continues to remind me that giving birth to anything takes time. For this man, our building project was a difficult birth, but in the end he became a proud parent.

# CHAPTER 10

# Planning with Motivation in Mind: The Deployment Step

*To note that effective planning must consider motives and values
is to return to our central emphasis on a general theory of political
leadership. Planning leaders, more than other leaders, must respond
not simply to popular attitudes and beliefs but to the fundamental
wants and needs, aspirations and expectations, values and goals of
their existing and potential followers.*[1]
—James MacGregor Burns

Congregants work to turn their vision into reality during deployment. This step commences once the congregation formally adopts a new direction for its future. In terms of the transtheoretical model, deployment takes the congregation from the preparation stage through the action stage to maintenance. Deployment ends when the goal is attained.

Good planning leads to a good experience during deployment. But planning should not be concerned only that the right actions are taken and the right resources are available to attain the goal. The probability of success increases in any change initiative when leaders acknowledge the motivational needs of congregants and plan to meet them during every stage of a change process.

Unfortunately, many congregational leaders fail to recognize and plan for members' motivational needs. A congregation in the United States lived for decades with a poorly designed building in an unattractive downtown location that had no parking. One day the leaders learned that a suburban sister congregation of their denomination was closing and would sell its church building. The leaders talked at length for months about the possibility of relocating to the other—and, they assumed, certainly better—facility. This building was well designed, was the right size for their congregation's needs, had lots of parking, was easily accessible and well maintained, and was located in the part of the city where most of their members lived. In addition, appraisals of the market value of both facilities led the leaders to believe that selling one facility to purchase the other one would net the congregation a significant profit. The leaders were convinced that relocation was the right idea.

So one Sunday at worship, the leaders informed the congregation of the idea—news to the congregation. The leaders then informed the congregation that next week's service would be held at the prospective new building so that everyone could experience it. Then the leaders told the congregation that the following Sunday—two weeks away—a congregational meeting would be held to decide whether the congregation would relocate. In other words, two weeks after the congregation heard about the idea for the first time, congregants would be asked to decide whether they would leave their home of eighty years. Worship attendance the following week at the potential new church building was the highest the congregation had seen in years. So too was attendance at the congregational meeting the week after, at which the majority said no to the proposal. The majority of the congregants were attached to their current building, despite its significant shortcomings, which were acknowledged by everyone. The leaders approached this issue in such a pragmatic way that they overlooked the significant motivational challenge they faced. Consequently, the leaders failed to plan for the congregational meeting with motivation in mind.

Failing to plan is planning to fail. Church consultant Kennon Callahan believes that the failure of congregational leaders to plan adequately for motivation is a common pitfall. He says that leaders are often motivated by challenge, reasonability, and commitment. In the example above, the leaders had a strong commitment to the future well-being of their congregation, understood the challenges of the present building, and knew that relocation was a reasonable solution to meet the challenges and improve the congregation's future.

But congregants often do not think like the leaders. Callahan writes, "One of the fatal mistakes some of us make is to assume that because we [church leaders] motivate ourselves in a certain way, we can help other people motivate themselves in the same way that we motivate ourselves. It is a fatal mistake."[2] In our example, the leaders assumed that the congregation shared the leaders' perspective, attitudes, and motives and would be motivated to approve the idea of relocation—a fatal mistake. "Failing to plan is planning to fail" applies as much to motivational issues as it does to timelines, budgets, resources, and to-do lists. Too many important goals and great plans fail because motivational concerns are not addressed.

The first motivational concern of planning is to build strategies for motivation into your plan, from the initial step of strengthening readiness to change right through to goal attainment. The five components of a change message is a scheme leaders should keep in mind while creating a motivating plan, since the plan, after all, effects what is promised in the change message. The second motivational concern of planning flows from the first: a plan is a change message in and of itself. Excellent plans strengthen congregants' hope that the goal is attainable by strengthening both their capability and context beliefs, as well as strengthening trust in the leaders.

## Picking Leaders with Motivation in Mind

Leadership books rarely include motivational considerations among the suggested criteria for choosing a leadership team for a change initiative. Bill Hybels, for instance, proposes his "three Cs": character (including a devotional Christian faith, honesty, teachability, humility, reliability, and a healthy work ethic), proven competence (giftedness and experience), and chemistry (team members' positive relational fit with each other).[3] John Kotter proposes four key characteristics for good team members: position power (include key, appropriate congregational leaders), expertise (ensure team members have the required abilities), guaranteed credibility (select a team congregants will trust), and leadership (seek people with the ability to "drive change," as Kotter puts it).[4] These are all excellent considerations, but only one of these seven selection criteria (credibility) given by these two noted leadership authors approaches a motivational concern. Hybels and Kotter are more interested in people being chosen based on their capability. Typically overlooked among such team-building lists are two other criteria: team members must be motivated, and they must be motivating. In fact, the absence of these last two criteria in a team member will undermine any strengths the person has in the first seven.

Look for team members who are motivated to participate in project leadership. Ask yourself the following questions when considering a potential candidate:

- Does the person already act like a steward of the present and future life of the congregation?
- Does the person share the concern for current reality that is a push motivation for action?
- Does the person have a goal-oriented nature? Not everyone does, and those who don't may not be focused and driven enough to apply their time, energy, giftedness, and experience.
- Does the person generally believe that congregational change is necessary for the future's sake? In other words, does the person already feel a pull motivation for action?
- Does the person have the strong personal capability beliefs needed for the task? People with strong capability beliefs are not easily discouraged when facing the trials of plan implementation. Instead, they tend to respond to challenges by increasing their efforts.
- Does the person have the strong personal context beliefs needed for the task? Does the person believe that the environment of the congregation will not prevent the congregation from attaining its goal?

Also look for team members who will be motivating for the congregation. The particular individuals who make up the leadership team for your congregation's change initiative will affect the congregation's confidence not only in the leaders but also in the achievability of the initiative. Consider your candidates for the leadership team using the three character qualities of trust-based relationships:

- Will congregants believe that this person has in his or her heart the best interests of the congregation?
- Will congregants believe that this person has the needed knowledge, gifts, and experience for this work?
- Will congregants see this person as reliable?

The more confidence congregants have in the project's leadership team, the more inclined congregants will be to accept change as important and sensible.

## Team Building with Motivation in Mind

A typical response when a congregation discovers a discrepancy gap is to create some kind of project or planning team to lead change. Picking team members with motivation in mind helps team effectiveness, but it is not the only motivational concern. Planning teams often believe they are going about their work objectively, but as the team clarifies the congregation's situation and develops goals and plans, they are also unconsciously reflecting on their own motives and attitudes. After all, motives and attitudes prompt people to have concerns regarding current reality, make one goal more appealing than other possible goals, and make specific plans seem sensible. If team members do not make a conscious effort to be aware of their own motivations when planning, then their motivations will take subconscious control of the planning process. Two negative effects may arise as a consequence. First, it may result in the team tumbling into Callahan's pitfall of assuming what motivates the leaders is also what motivates the congregation. This pitfall easily leads to the second negative effect: making plans without motivation in mind.

Teams can avoid these negative effects and engage in some initial team building by sharing their own personal motives and attitudes regarding the discrepancy gap and for their participation in the project. At the team's first meeting the convener simply asks members to introduce themselves and then state why they agreed to be on the team. This question opens the doors for people to express their own motives and attitudes about the team's project. The exercise strengthens the bonds of a team because team members will probably discover that they substantially share the same concerns and hopes about the discrepancy gap, which represents shared motivation. The exercise will probably also highlight individual motivations as well. For example, imagine a congregation that forms a team to create a new ministry for the homeless people in its neighborhood. One team member might share that her brother was homeless for a period and speak about the impact that had on her family. Her motivation is a value to help those who are homeless and her compassion for those in need arising from her experience. Other team members, hearing this motive, will likely feel empathy and greater solidarity with this individual. Empathy, which is the vicarious experience of the feelings of another person, helps us adopt the motives of others that were not first our own.

The agenda of a project team's first meeting tends to be dominated by defining and understanding more fully the team's purpose, giving the team some organizational shape, and engaging in some preliminary planning. If the discrepancy gap is already well defined, then it may also be helpful to conduct an initial round of the force field analysis exercise in order to introduce to the team the importance of maintaining awareness of congregational motivation. After all, the congregation had some motives and attitudes for creating the team in the first place, and congregants expect the team to represent these motives and attitudes through its work. The exercise could focus on the question, Why would our congregation want—and not want—to deal with this discrepancy gap? Through the exercise, team members will develop an initial appreciation of the congregation's drivers and resisters for the project and perhaps begin to see that some congregational motives and attitudes are different from their own. This initial consciousness-raising exercise can help team members be more mindful of congregational motivation throughout the duration of their work together.

## Articulating Goals with Motivation in Mind

We tend to think of goals only as clear, objective statements that describe what people want to attain, but goals by their nature and construction are also motivating in and of themselves. They direct our attention and govern our choices. They help foster commitment, encourage effort, as well as prompt persistence in attainment. As seen in chapter 2, goals have several motivating characteristics, and the more these qualities can be built into the definition of a goal or vision, the more motivating it will be. Ideally a goal is

- specific and clear: to help direct action;
- high and attainable: to motivate people to strive harder;
- immediate: to generate urgency; and
- necessary: to explain the crucial motives for pursuing the goal.

Other characteristics also help make a goal or vision for the future more motivating, such as describing the goal in positive language ("Our goal is to equal last year's financial success"), rather than in negative language ("Our goal is not to do worse than last year"). Motivation is strengthened when the goal is described in ways that are pertinent and meaningful for the congregation—in terms that capture congregational motivations, stories, and identity. Finally, a goal is more motivating when it is the congregation's only goal, or one of only a few goals. Presenting too many or too disparate goals reduces congregational focus and diminishes the motivating power of goals. Choosing only the most necessary goals focuses congregational energy and activity.

## Developing Plans with Motivation in Mind

Solid plans motivate congregants by strengthening their capability and context beliefs. Solid plans assure the congregation that the goal is attainable and that the resources needed to attain the goal (including funding, human resources, time, and effort) will be available. Stronger plans make for a stronger change message that will inspire greater confidence in congregants, not only in the project itself but also in the congregation's leaders. A solid plan also builds the confidence of the project leaders because it strengthens the capability and context beliefs they will need to maintain their motivation through plan implementation. What follows is a comprehensive checklist for creating solid plans. Depending on your situation, you may not need to use every element listed below, but the list is provided to help you think through what might be required.

## Consider Participative Planning

Invite those who will share responsibility for plan implementation to participate in developing the plan itself, because participation strengthens goal commitment and motivation during implementation. Participation has this effect because people generally design plans they believe they can accomplish. In other words, people are tacitly guided by their capability beliefs. So when planners complete their work and say to themselves, "We can do this!" they feel empowered and motivated to achieve what they believe they can do. Participation also strengthens motivation because it creates ownership of the plan, which usually translates into a greater sense of responsibility for its achievement.

## Clearly State the Goal and Its Rationale

A well-articulated goal is motivating in and of itself, but the rationale for the goal is also motivating because it describes the congregation's motives for pursuing the goal. The project team must be clear about both the goal and its rationale, since the team's task is to lead goal attainment, and congregants will expect the team to satisfy their motives for the project. Also, as we've seen above, it is motivating for team members to articulate their own personal motives for pursuing the goal.

## Create Clear Objectives

As we saw in chapter 2, broad, vague goals decrease motivation because they lack clarity. That being said, sometimes the overall goal simply has to be quite general. This problem is overcome by breaking the broad goal down into a series of more specific objectives, which is a planning practice that brings motivational advantages. Objectives provide people with the needed specificity to focus attention and effort. They break a large goal into manageable tasks people believe they can do, strengthening capability and context beliefs. Clear objectives also create the framework for focused and effective feedback during implementation. A sense of urgency can also be created when the scope of objectives is relatively limited, so the time and effort required to attain them is relatively short.

Authors Robert Craig and Robert Worley in their book *Dry Bones Live* provide an excellent description of what makes for a well-defined objective.[5] Objectives should have the following features:

- Goal-directed. The objective can be clearly seen as a necessary step toward attaining the overarching goal.
- Understandable. Clarity and specificity helps people know exactly what they need to do.
- Assignable. People will know clearly what they have to do.
- Achievable. People will be able to visualize the objective as attainable with the available resources.
- Measurable. The objective will help people know whether they are succeeding during implementation and when the objective is attained.
- Controllable. The objective is defined clearly enough to minimize surprises or distractions.

When objectives are defined in these ways, they make not only planning but also the management of plan implementation easier.

## Set Target Dates

Open-ended timelines tend to let projects drag on. Setting due dates for the overall goal and the different objectives ensures that a degree of urgency will focus effort. Deadlines also reinforce people's sense of responsibility. They also help ensure that those who need to wait for the attainment of one objective in a sequence are not left frustrated.

## Outline Project Management Structure

Some projects can be pretty complicated. A building project, for example, involves task groups for design development, construction oversight, fund-raising, and communicating, and the work of each group affects the others. Clarifying, integrating, streamlining, and managing the relationships between task groups helps minimize demotivating frustrations. A simple organizational chart detailing responsibilities and paths of accountability clarifies people's roles, which in turn helps maintain capability beliefs. A project management structure also ensures that those with top-level responsibility are kept abreast of progress and have the needed information to coordinate the project overall.

## Plan for Communications

There are two kinds of communications needs during a major project: internal and external. Planners should ask the following questions:

- What communication structures and habits does each task group need to help the internal functioning of the task group?
- Whom does the task group need to communicate with beyond its membership: Project leaders? Congregational leaders? The congregation itself? The lead minister? The staff? Other task groups? Stakeholder groups in the congregation?
- What needs to be communicated when?

A good communication plan helps plan implementation.

## Plan for Resources

A plan that organizes resources well strengthens capability and context beliefs. Planners need to be mindful of the following:

- Budget and financial resources. How much money is needed by each task group in order to support the attainment of its objectives on schedule? Budgeting a contingency fund "just in case" strengthens confidence that this necessary resource will truly be adequate and available. Conversely, the tighter the budget, the more anxious people may become.

- Material resources. The task group may rely on others to provide needed material resources, such as craft supplies, lumber, or a pickup truck. Plan to have needed materials arrive on schedule.
- People resources. Implementation goes smoothly when the right people participate the right way at the right time. People resources can be strengthened in the following ways:

  - Knowledge support. What information might this group need to help it pursue its objective?
  - Training support. What skills or experience might this group need to acquire to help it pursue its objective?
  - Oversight support. What kind of management, evaluation, feedback, and encouragement might this group need to help it pursue its objective?

People who know they are well supported have stronger capability and context beliefs and will feel more motivated as a consequence.

## Planning Feedback with Motivation in Mind

Feedback informs people about their progress toward their objective. What the project team will measure to assess progress, how often that measurement needs to be taken and reported, and how the feedback will be used by the project leaders are all important questions to ask when planning. Understanding how progress will be determined is an important aspect of solid planning, but feedback also has a critical effect on motivation. Capability beliefs ("We can do this!") and context beliefs ("Our setting will allow us to do this!") are simply that: beliefs. These beliefs tend to remain stable until they are strengthened or diminished by experience. During plan implementation, feedback unavoidably provides real-time evidence to either support or challenge these beliefs, which in turn will strengthen or weaken motivation.

For example, let's say congregants set a goal to increase the number of younger adults in the congregation. A few changes are made to improve the congregation's appeal to this age group. Progress toward the goal is measured by the change in the number of younger adults in the congregation—the feedback. If the number of people in this age group doesn't increase, then the feedback is telling the congregation that those few changes were not effective for attaining their goal and that other strategies should be considered. But negative feedback typically affects motivation as well. Lack of success often leaves congregants demoralized. Congregants could interpret the feedback this way: "No matter what we do, we won't be able to attract the next generation, because they aren't interested in going to church." A negative attitude like this one leads to weakened context beliefs, which easily puts an end to further efforts to appeal to younger adults. Conversely, if the number of young adults begins to increase significantly, then the feedback is telling the congregation that they have a successful strategy. This feedback, in turn, will enhance motivation by strengthening capability and context beliefs, since the evidence demonstrates that the congregation is able to appeal to this demographic group. Feedback affects motivation. Consequently, leaders need to think through how to manage feedback to either protect capability and context beliefs—which were needed in this illustration—or strengthen them to improve motivation.

Leaders support people's motivation by encouraging the recipients of demoralizing feedback to use it to reconsider the plan, which helps protect the goal and people's sense of self. They focus attention on the plan by asking questions such as, Do we need to change the way we are implementing our plan? Do we have to make adjustments to our plan? or even, Does the feedback suggest the need for a different strategy so that we can attain our goal? Focus is also directed toward the plan when leaders intentionally direct attention away from the goal (by reaffirming the importance of the goal) and away from people's sense of self (by acknowledging their hard work, affirming their abilities, and pointing out that the issues lie with the plan and not with the people).

Ensuring that feedback is properly directed starts in planning by being clear and up front about the form feedback will take, what will be measured, and what will be evaluated by those measures. Let people know from the beginning that feedback is only about progress toward the goal. Leaders also help congregants by listening to people's reactions to the feedback to hear where they direct it and by redirecting it away from the goal or themselves and toward its proper target: the strategy and what is being done to effect the strategy. Leaders also protect participants by deflecting people from "the blame game," such as attributing lack of progress to the poor effort of some team members, perceived bad attitudes, some people's temperament, and so on, since this behavior also weakens motivation.

The language used in feedback also affects motivation. When possible, present the data in positive terms ("We've found ten volunteers!") rather than in negative terms ("We still need to find ten more volunteers"). Also frame feedback in encouraging terms whenever possible ("You made that look easier than it actually was. Good work!"). When progress is made, help people reflect on their own capability and context beliefs so that those beliefs become stronger. Good quality feedback not only gets people through the current project but also strengthens their context and capability beliefs for the next project and the one after that.

But remember: be honest, because people aren't stupid. Disappointing feedback that is sugarcoated is still what it is—disappointing—and people will see past the coating. The reality is that some objectives are hard to attain, and the elements of some plans are difficult to effect. Consequently, it is doubly critical to think about people's capability and context beliefs. At this point leaders may need to help team members step back and draw on other sources to maintain context and capability beliefs: people's past successes in somewhat similar projects, how other congregations managed to get through this same tough spot as they moved on to succeed in the same goal, or how God is supporting them. At some point, leaders may also find it necessary to rethink the chosen strategy of the plan and to look for other potential strategies that could work better. A new strategy may rejuvenate flagging motivation by renewing capability and context beliefs.

## Contingency Planning with Motivation in Mind

The Scottish poet Robert Burns was quite right when he wrote that "the best laid schemes of mice and men go oft awry." We know from life experience that things don't always work out as planned, and our appreciation of this reality actually creates motivational issues. During planning congregants may conceive several ways to attain the goal, which may cause uncertainty regarding which path is best. Then, once on a chosen path, not every factor in the plan may be under the control of the project team, which may also create uncertainty. Regardless of its origins, uncertainty diminishes motivation.

Uncertainty can be decreased and confidence strengthened by planning for contingencies. Contingency planning asks, What if this bit here doesn't go as expected? and subsequently prepares for that possibility. It is best conducted in advance of implementation, when the considerations are only theoretical "what ifs." Contingency planning strengthens motivation by making plans stronger and thus easier to trust. It also strengthens capability and context beliefs, because people have considered and planned for different scenarios brought about by uncontrollable elements of the plan.

Contingency planning is also a great opportunity to think about the future motivational needs of the congregation. Ask questions such as these:

- Are there any moments during implementation when the congregation might see its enthusiasm lag and motivation decline? If so, what can we do about it?
- What could distract our congregation from following through on our plans?
- What do we do if people start shifting back into old habits?

By planning to deal with the uncontrollable and anticipating the unexpected, leaders reduce uncertainties and bolster confidence.

## Planning with the Late Adopters and Resistant in Mind

As we saw in chapter 4, diffusion theory tells us that late adopters need more time than others to appreciate, accept, and adopt change. Leaders should plan for the needs of late adopters, since we know late adopters must see evidence of the project's merits emerging during implementation. Leaders can ask, What will late adopters need to reduce their skepticism about this initiative, and how can we build into our plan the evidence they require? During plan implementation, leaders need to treat the resistant as if they were late adopters, with the hope that as the needs of late adopters are met, some of the resistant may join in as well.

A communications plan for late adopters is also helpful. If the leaders know the evidence late adopters are looking for, then they can let them know when that milestone will be reached. Some late adopters dislike and wish to avoid the feelings of stress that the uncertainty of change inevitably creates. These people need a steady diet of project updates shaped to communicate confidence, progress, and success. Other congregants may still be worried that aspects of congregational life they have been told will not change in actuality will change, and they fear its loss. Leaders can plan occasions that prove these fears are not warranted. Finally, if something can be done to mitigate or compensate for actual loss, then as a sign of good faith, leaders should plan to enact these adjustments as soon as they can.

## Planning the End of the Project with Motivation in Mind

Congregants may be tempted to mark the completion of a project by simply going home because everyone is tired, but that will result in a missed motivational opportunity the celebration of success brings. Fulfilling a vision should strengthen people's capability and context beliefs, but this benefit of success is not always recognized and marked in some way. If it is, then the success of one project gives congregants greater confidence for the next project. Leaders can help congregants strengthen their capability and context beliefs by highlighting that congregants

- entered into the project knowing their abilities would be challenged, and success proved the congregation's ability to rise to the challenge;
- went into the project hoping that their context wouldn't be a barrier to success, and they learned that it wasn't;

- kept this project before God in prayer, hoping for support, so in success gratitude needs to be given to God for the help received;
- learned they were a stronger congregation than they might first have imagined; and
- demonstrated to themselves that they are good stewards of the congregation's future and that the congregation to follow will be grateful for what was done on its behalf.

Do not relegate these encouragements to the final party alone. The legacy of success is best remembered in the congregation's story so that the capability and context beliefs will continue to strengthen congregational motivation. Success in any endeavor in congregational life is, after all, an act of faithfulness. Encourage congregants to recall and retell their stories of success in ways that affirm their abilities so that they will have greater trust in their abilities the next time.

This outline of motivational concerns in planning is not comprehensive. The distinctiveness of every congregation, goal, and plan will suggest unique motivational opportunities for the deployment step that leaders should anticipate and build into their plans. If leaders maintain a perspective that planning for congregational motivation is as important as planning for goal attainment, however, then they will be more confident that the congregation will not simply weather change but thrive through it.

# Afterword

What is leadership? Leadership is stewardship of the well-being of a community in the present and for its future. Leadership is a role a community confers to those they entrust with that stewardship. The leaders' task, in part, is to discern new common goals and then to help others of the community understand them, embrace them, and pursue them. At its core today, leadership is about helping people choose to do something new that will make the community more authentic, meaningful, vital, and able. In an era of personal choice, leadership has become more and more about encouraging and facilitating faithful choice making for the future, which will lead to new intentions and actions in the community. To enact such leadership, leaders need to appreciate motivation as both a science and an art. They also need to recognize that motivational leadership is a practice that takes practice.

Some people reduce motivation to base appeals: pandering, inciting fear, or inducing guilt. At this level, motivation too easily slides into manipulation, and people quickly spot it for what it is. Others think motivation is about rhetoric, such as locker-room speeches and roll-outs such as pep rallies. While great speeches are highly influential in the moment, they frequently do not have sufficient staying power to maintain motivation through the often prolonged process of change. A great speech is only a condiment for the motivational main course, which is influencing motives, attitudes, and intentions whenever opportunity arises.

Perhaps this book was not what you expected. We've covered a lot of substance—theories and concepts—perhaps more than you bargained for! You might also think this book is more about engineering change rather than inspiring change. The reality is that the psychology of motivation is a complex but necessary science. I say "necessary science" quite deliberately, because we live in an age when the need for change is all around us in our society, not just within the church. To face long-term concerns such as growing environmental problems, the legacy of deficit budgets by governments, social welfare issues, the tragedies of developing nations and so on, leaders must influence people to move beyond the motives of short-term self-interest so that we as a society will embrace a greater stewardship of our future. The science of motivation is a crucial tool for this task. But it is also an art, since influence depends on appreciating the sense of reality or the worldview of diverse people and the motives and attitudes behind their perspectives, and then discerning how to appeal to those motives and attitudes in different ways that help people choose to change.

This book was written with two premises in mind. First, if we choose to lead change, then we must appreciate the power of choice people have today. Second, if we wish to influence those choices, we must understand human nature and how thoughts, feelings, habits, motives, attitudes, and intentions all influence people to change. Ours is a society in which we define ourselves by the choices we have made, are making, and will make. If we as leaders hope to influence the people of our communities to make faithful and helpful choices for our futures, then we need to understand the complicated workings of human motivation. And much more than just the sustainability of our congregations is at stake. In the Sermon on the Mount, Jesus calls congregations "the light of the world," "a city built on a hill [that] cannot be hid," and "the salt of the earth." Faith communities are called to be visible, life-giving change agents in the world. "Let your light shine before others, so that they may see your good works and give glory to your Father in heaven" (Matt. 5:13–16), Jesus taught. To be faithful in this calling, we must first be open to choose change ourselves. Then, if we choose change, perhaps we can be part of the remedy for the ills of our age.

Fortunately, a growing number of congregations are making this choice, and the change they are embracing often goes to the heart of their understanding of the calling and nature of the church. It seems to me that the ecclesiologies that have nurtured and sustained the church in the past have been found wanting by many and discarded by some.

New ecclesiologies—the purpose-driven church, the missional church, the house church movement, the emerging church, new monasticism, postevangelicalism, and the practicing congregation—have arrived. I'm sure there are many others as well. For leaders to effect congregational change today, their role at times is to be midwives for the birth of a new ecclesiology, one that includes different beliefs and attitudes about the nature of a congregation. Like in human births—when the gender of the infant is not known until the baby's arrival—leaders may not know the nature of the new ecclesiology until it has come to life in a congregation. But when it does, bringing new, relevant meaning and vitality to a faith community, then the congregation will know in new ways the life in abundance promised by Jesus, and it will shine bright as the light to the world.

I've just claimed that the situation the church finds itself in today is new, which is both true and not true. The story of the church shows that people of faith have always seen and accepted the challenge to change. We need think only of the mind-boggling diversity of the church today as compared with the way it looked on the day of Pentecost. But despite the diversity, the highest aspirations of communities of faith have always been the same, which is to be

- faithful to our Lord Jesus Christ,
- authentic as the body of Christ,
- aligned with the *missio Dei*,
- significant to the people who make up the faith community,
- relevant to the needs of the wider society, and
- intentional in service of others, as good stewards of the manifold grace of God.

Thus it has always been. But in our day these aspirations seem to us more challenging, given what appears to many people as the sudden arrival of rapid societal change. Such change has left many congregations wondering how they will cope, let alone evolve. But imagine what a congregation would look like as it rises to meet these aspirations!

The long-term challenges that congregational leaders face today are significant, and this book is but one of many written in recent years to help leaders in these times. As you have read this book in particular,

I hope it has strengthened your capability beliefs. This book provides you with a collection of tools to expand your understanding of motivation in the practice of leadership. I believe that leaders equipped with these tools will be more effective in their work. As you put these tools to use, be mindful of your experience in leadership and learn from it, and you will find your own capability beliefs growing as a consequence.

I hope that this book has also strengthened your context beliefs. As congregations face challenges, the task of helping congregants engage in significant change may appear quite daunting to leaders. Leaders may wonder how much influence they really have, which is a context belief. After all, the most significant context of a leader's work is the congregation itself. But, generally, the answer from the field of motivation psychology regarding how much influence leaders have is this: more than you might think. The material in this book is a primer for understanding your context for leadership. If you understand generally why and how people make the choices they do, then you understand your context, and your influence will increase. That being said, people will not always make the choice you hope they will make. After all, in our faith communities we deal with people trained by society to believe they have an autonomous right to make their own choices. But knowing how those choices are made gives leaders an inside edge. And again, as you put this knowledge to use, mindful of your experience in leadership and learning from it, you will find your context beliefs growing stronger as well.

Finally, I hope you will apply this book in other areas of ministry in addition to leading congregational change. The ideas of this book inform my sermon preparation, because like all preachers, I hope that my preaching will be influential. These concepts inform my work in pastoral care, because like all pastors, I hope to help people navigate the transitions of their lives from brokenness to wholeness. They inform my approach as a Christian educator, because like all clergy, I hope to help people deepen their relationship with God and follow more closely after Jesus Christ as disciples. They guide my work as a missional leader, because like all church leaders, I aspire to see the congregation I serve have a greater impact on our wider community for the sake of the kingdom of God.

Whether we recognize it or not, clergy are in the change business in virtually everything we do. Consequently, understanding motivation can make a difference in virtually everything we do.

May God bless you in all you do.

# Notes

1. "Pastoral Study Project Program," The Louisville Institute website, http://www.louisville-institute.org/Grants/programs/pspdetail.aspx.

## Chapter 1, What Is Motivation and Why Is It Important?

1. John C. Maxwell, *The 21 Most Powerful Minutes in a Leader's Day* (Nashville: Thomas Nelson, 2000), 17.
2. Albert Bandura, *Self-Efficacy: The Exercise of Control* (New York: W. H. Freeman, 1997), 228.
3. Peter L. Berger, "A Market Model for the Analysis of Ecumenicity," *Social Research* (1963): 77–93.
4. Wade Clark Roof and William McKinney, *American Mainline Religion* (New Brunswick, NJ: Rutgers University Press, 1987), 40.
5. Wade Clark Roof, *Spiritual Marketplace: Baby Boomers and the Remaking of American Religion* (Princeton, NJ: Princeton University Press, 1999).
6. Ibid., 49.
7. Martin E. P. Seligman, *Learned Optimism: How to Change Your Mind and Your Life* (New York: Vintage Books, 2006), 20.
8. Eric Reed, "Leadership Surveys Church Conflict," *Leadership Journal,* Fall 2004.
9. Johannes van der Ven, *Ecclesiology in Context* (Grand Rapids: Eerdmans, 1996), 444.
10. Ibid., 443.

11. For a comprehensive treatment of these ideas, see Robert Wuthnow's book *After Heaven: Spirituality in America since the 1950s* (Berkeley: University of California Press, 1998).

12. Jackson Carroll, *God's Potters: Pastoral Leadership and the Shaping of Congregations* (Grand Rapids: William B. Eerdmans, 2006), 270.

13. Ibid., 145–51. My thanks to Dr. Carroll for his assistance in this reinterpretation of his data.

14. Ibid., 258.

## Chapter 2, Stewardship and Hope at Work

1. Kurt Lewin, *Field Theory in Social Science: Selected Theoretical Papers* (New York: Harper & Row, 1951), 169.

2. Gabriele Oettingen and Elizabeth J. Stephens, "Fantasies and Motivationally Intelligent Goal Setting" in *The Psychology of Goals,* ed. Gordon B. Moskowitz and Heidi Grant (New York: The Guilford Press),153–78.

3. Joseph Cesario, E. Tory Higgins, and Abigail A. Scholer, "Regulatory Fit and Persuasion: Basic Principles and Remaining Questions," *Social and Personality Psychology Compass* 2, no. 1 (2008): 444–63.

4. Bill Hybels, *Courageous Leadership* (Grand Rapids: Zondervan, 2002), 33.

5. Bill Hybels, *Holy Discontent: Fueling the Fire That Ignites Personal Vision* (Grand Rapids: Zondervan, 2007), 24–25.

6. Edgar H. Schein, *The Corporate Culture Survival Guide* (San Francisco: Jossey-Bass, 2009), 116–17.

7. This approach to understanding motivation is adopted from the theory of reasoned action. A comprehensive treatment of the theory is found in Martin Fishbein and Icek Ajzen, *Predicting and Changing Behavior: The Reasoned Action Approach* (New York: Psychology Press, 2010).

8. Rune Lines, "The Structure and Function of Attitudes toward Organizational Change," *Human Resource Development Review* 4, no. 1 (2005): 8–32.

9. Fishbein and Ajzen, *Predicting and Changing Behavior*, 39.

10. TV interview of Prime Minister Margaret Thatcher by Brian Walden for London Weekend Television *Weekend World*, January 6, 1980. Text from Margaret Thatcher Foundation website, http://www.margaretthatcher.org/speeches/displaydocument. asp?docid=104210.

11. Peter M. Gollwitzer, "Implementation Intentions: Strong Effects of Simple Plans," *American Psychologist* 54, no. 7 (July 1999): 493–503.

12. Diana Butler Bass, *The Practicing Congregation* (Herndon, VA: Alban Institute, 2004), 80, emphasis in original.

## Chapter 3, Trust at Work

1. From the pamphlet *Wellspring* (n.p., n.d.) as quoted in Estelle Avery Sharpe, *Foundation Stones of Success,* vol. 3, *Conversational Lessons on Social Ethics* (Chicago: Howard-Severance, 1910), 24.

2. This chapter draws on the work of Albert Bandura and others who have built on his theories. His landmark publication is the six-hundred-page book *Self-Efficacy: The Exercise of Control* (New York: W. H. Freeman, 1997). This comprehensive book explores the role of personal efficacy beliefs (what I call capability beliefs) not only in organizational change but also in such diverse issues as the effectiveness of students and teachers, depression, athleticism, addictions, health promotion, international development, aging, eating disorders, and phobias. A summary of the book is found in the chapter "Personal and Collective Efficacy in Human Adaptation and Change," in *Advances in Psychological Science*, vol. 1, *Personal, Social and Cultural Aspects*, ed. J. G. Adair, D. Belanger, and K. L. Dion (Hove, UK: Psychology Press, 1998), http://www.uky.edu/~eushe2/ Bandura/Bandura1998Change.pdf. Another excellent summary is "Cultivate Self-Efficacy for Personal and Organizational Effectiveness," in *Handbook of Principles of Organization Behavior*, ed. E. A. Locke (Hoboken, NJ: Blackwell, 2000), and found at http://www.uky.edu/~eushe2/Bandura/Bandura2000.pdf.

3. Peter Guralnick, *Last Train to Memphis: The Rise of Elvis Presley* (London: Little Brown, 1994), 77.
4. John Kotter, *Leading Change* (Boston: Harvard Business School Press, 1996), 35–49.
5. Gary Latham, *Work Motivation: History, Theory, Research, and Practice* (Thousand Oaks, CA: Sage, 2007), 231–32.
6. Ibid., 231–37.

**Chapter 4, Motivation-Based Change**

1. Ronald Heifetz, *Leadership without Easy Answers* (Cambridge, MA: The Belknap Press of Harvard University Press, 1994), 14.
2. Peter Senge, Charlotte Roberts, Rick Ross, and Bryan Smith, *The Dance of Change: The Challenges to Sustaining Momentum in Learning Organizations* (New York: Currency Doubleday, 1999), 5–6.
3. W. Warner Burke, *Organization Change: Theory and Practice* (Thousand Oaks, CA: Sage Publications, 2008), 11.
4. Senge et al., *Dance of Change*, 6.
5. James Prochaska and Carlo C. DiClemente, "Stages and Processes of Self-change of Smoking: Toward an Integrative Model of Change," *Journal of Consulting and Clinical Psychology* 51, no. 3 (June 1983): 390–95.
6. Martin Fishbein and Icek Ajzen, *Predicting and Changing Behavior: The Reasoned Action Approach* (New York: Psychology Press, 2010): 353–57.
7. Ibid.
8. Everett M. Rogers, *Diffusion of Innovations* (New York: Free Press, 2003), chap. 7.
9. Ibid., xv–xvi.
10. Ibid., 273.
11. Figures obtained from Internet World Stats: Usage and Population Statistics, http://www.internetworldstats.com/facebook.htm. Used by permission. Copyright © 2012, Miniwatts Marketing Group. All rights reserved worldwide.
12. Shayndi Raice, "Days of Wild User Growth Appear Over at Facebook," *The Wall Street Journal*, June 11, 2012,

http://online.wsj.com/article/SB10001424052702303296604577
454970244896342.html.

13. Janice M. Prochaska, James O. Prochaska, and Deborah A.
Levesque, "A Transtheoretical Approach to Changing Organizations," *Administration and Policy in Mental Health* 28, no. 4
(March 2001): 247–61.

14. Max DePree, *Leadership Is an Art* (New York: Dell, 1989), xix.
Capital letter and italics are DePree's.

15. Heifetz, *Leadership without Easy Answers*, 87.

## Chapter 5, Preparing the Congregation

1. John Kotter, *Leading Change* (Boston: Harvard Business School
Press, 1996), 17–18.

2. Achilles Armenakis, Stanley Harris, and Kevin Mossholder,
"Creating Readiness for Organizational Change," *Human Relations* 46, no. 6 (June 1993): 681–703.

3. Daniel Holt, Achilles Armenakis, Stanley Harris, and Hubert
Field, "Toward a Comprehensive Definition of Readiness for
Change: A Review of Research and Instrumentation," *Research
in Organizational Change and Development* 16, ed. William
Passmore and R. W. Woodman (Oxford: Elsevier, 2007): 295–
346.

4. Morela Hernandez, "Promoting Stewardship Behavior in Organizations: A Leadership Model," *Journal of Business Ethics* 80,
no. 1 (2008): 121–22.

5. Kimberly Wade-Benzoni, "Giving Future Generations a Voice,"
in *The Negotiator's Fieldbook: The Desk Reference for the Experienced Negotiator,* ed. Andrea Schneider and Christopher Honeyman (Washington, DC: American Bar Association, 2006),
215–23.

6. Kimberly Wade-Benzoni, "A Golden Rule over Time: Reciprocity in Intergenerational Allocation Decisions," *Academy of
Management Journal* 45, no. 5 (October 2002): 1011–28.

7. Kimberly Wade-Benzoni, "Legacies, Immortality, and the Future: The Psychology of Intergenerational Altruism," *Research
on Managing Groups and Teams* 8 (2006): 247–70.

8. Ibid., 255.
9. Reginald Bibby, *Beyond the Gods and Back: Religion's Demise and Rise and Why It Matters* (Lethbridge, AB: Project Canada Books, 2011), 45.
10. Roger C. Mayer, James H. Davis, and F. David Schoorman, "An Integrative Model of Organizational Trust," *The Academy of Management Review* 20, no. 3 (1995): 709–34.

## Chapter 6, Encouraging Attitude Change

1. Ogden Nash, *You Can't Get There from Here* (London: Little Brown Group, 1984).
2. Kennon L. Callahan, *Twelve Keys to an Effective Church* (San Francisco: HarperSanFrancisco, 1983), xii.
3. The World Café website, www.theworldcafe.com. Juanita Brown and David Isaacs, *The World Café: Shaping Our Futures through Conversations That Matter* (San Francisco: Berrett-Koehler Publishers, 2005).
4. *Café to Go* (The World Café, 2008), 4, http://www.theworldcafe.com/pdfs/cafetogo.pdf.
5. The Appreciative Inquiry Commons can be found at www.appreciativeinquiry.case.edu.
6. David Cooperrider and Diana Whitney, *Appreciative Inquiry: A Positive Revolution in Change* (San Francisco: Berrett-Koehler, 2005), 25–35.
7. Here the Narrative Leadership Collection of books from the Alban Institute can be very helpful, especially the book *Finding Our Story: Narrative Leadership and Congregational Change,* edited by Larry A. Goleman (2009).
8. Martin Fishbein and Icek Ajzen, *Predicting and Changing Behavior: The Reasoned Action Approach* (New York: Psychology Press, 2010), 243.
9. The Sesquicentennial History Committee, *Sesquicentennial History 1844–1994: Knox Presbyterian Church* (Guelph, ON: Knox Presbyterian Church, 1994), 51–52.

10. Thomas H. Groome, *Sharing Faith: A Comprehensive Approach to Religious Education and Pastoral Ministry* (San Francisco: HarperSanFrancisco, 1991), 146–48.
11. Ibid., 147.
12. Fishbein and Ajzen, *Predicting and Changing Behavior*, 261.
13. Edgar H. Schein, *The Corporate Culture Survival Guide* (San Francisco: Jossey-Bass, 1999), 121.

## Chapter 7, Developing the Change Story Together

1. Howard Gardner, *Changing Minds: The Art and Science of Changing Our Own and Other People's Minds* (Boston: Harvard Business School Press, 2006), 1.
2. Peter M. Senge, Art Kleiner, Charlotte Roberts, Richard B. Ross, and Bryan J. Smith, *The Fifth Discipline Fieldbook* (New York: Crown Business Random House, 1994), 312–26.
3. Jackson Carroll, *God's Potters: Pastoral Leadership and the Shaping of Congregations* (Grand Rapids: William B. Eerdmans, 2006), 132.
4. The ideas in this section are drawn from Ronald Heifetz, *Leadership without Easy Answers* (Cambridge, MA: The Belknap Press of Harvard University Press,1994), 69–124. Heifetz is the Senior Lecturer in Public Leadership at the John F. Kennedy School of Government of Harvard University. His background as a psychiatrist has influenced greatly his understanding of how to help people engage in change. *Leadership without Easy Answers* should be required reading for anyone at all serious about congregational leadership.
5. Ibid., 103–6.
6. Ibid., 138–39.
7. Ibid., 139–41.
8. Ibid., 141–42.
9. Ibid., 161.
10. Ibid., 113.
11. Ibid., 142–44.
12. Ibid., 144.

13. Jerome Bruner, "Life as Narrative" in *Social Research* 71, no. 3 (Fall 2004): 694.
14. Joseph Campbell, *Hero with a Thousand Faces* (New York: Pantheon Books, 1949).
15. Wendy Wood, "Attitude Change: Persuasion and Social Influence," *Annual Review of Psychology* 51 (2000): 551.
16. Gardner, *Changing Minds, 163.*

## Chapter 8, Crafting and Sharing the Change Message

1. Richard M. Perloff, *The Dynamics of Persuasion: Communication and Attitudes in the 21st Century*, 3rd ed. (New York: Routledge, 2008), 17.
2. Howard Gardner, *Changing Minds: The Art and Science of Changing Our Own and Other People's Minds* (Boston: Harvard Business School Press, 2006), 163.
3. Achilles A. Armenakis and Stanley G. Harris, "Crafting a Change Message to Create Transformational Readiness," *Journal of Organizational Change Management* 15, no. 2 (2002): 169–83.
4. Barbara L. Fredrickson, *Positivity: Top-Notch Research Reveals the 3-to-1 Ratio That Will Change Your Life* (New York: Crown Archetype, 2009), and David L. Cooperrider, Diana Whitney, and Jacqueline M. Stavros, *Appreciative Inquiry Handbook: For Leaders of Change*, 2nd ed. (San Francisco: Berrett-Koehler Publishers, 2008).
5. See John Kotter, *A Sense of Urgency* (Boston: Harvard Business School, 2008), and Edgar H. Schein, *The Corporate Culture Survival Guide* (San Francisco: Jossey-Bass, 2009), 116–17.
6. Armenakis and Harris, "Crafting a Change Message," 170.
7. Perloff, *Dynamics of Persuasion*, 249.
8. Ibid., 240.
9. Lambert Deckers, *Motivation: Biological, Psychological, and Environmental*, 2nd ed. (Boston: Pearson Education, 2005), 391–92.
10. Al Gore, *An Inconvenient Truth*. Directed by Davis Guggenheim (Los Angeles: Paramount Pictures, 2006).

11. Nelson Mandela's opening statement at his trial in response to the charges of sabotage, high treason, and conspiracy to over-throw the government, April 20, 1964. The History Place, Great Speeches Collection, http://www.historyplace.com/speeches/mandela.htm.
12. Randy Pausch, *The Last Lecture: Really Achieving Your Child-hood Dreams*, given at Carnegie Mellon University, September 18, 2007, http://www.youtube.com/watch?v=ji5_MqicxSo.
13. Perloff, *Dynamics of Persuasion*, 408–9.
14. President Barack Obama's Inaugural Address, January 20, 2009, The White House Blog website, http://www.whitehouse.gov/blog/inaugural-address.

## Chapter 9, Dealing with Dissent

1. James O'Toole, *Leading Change: The Argument for Values-Based Leadership* (New York: Ballantine Books, 1996), 189.
2. John Stuart Mill, *On Liberty and Other Writings* (Cambridge, UK: The Press Syndicate of the University of Cambridge, 1989), 70.
3. Russell Cropanzano, Zinta S. Byrne, D. Ramona Bobocel, and Deborah E. Rupp, "Moral Virtues, Fairness Heuristics, Social Entities, and Other Denizens of Organizational Justice," *Journal of Vocational Behavior* 58, no. 2 (2001): 164–209.
4. Martin Fishbein and Icek Ajzen, *Predicting and Changing Be-havior: The Reasoned Action Approach* (New York: Psychology Press, 2010), 243.
5. O'Toole, *Leading Change*, 254.
6. This exercise follows the philosophy of the theory of constraints, which was developed by Eliyahu Goldratt. An approachable introduction to his work is his novel *The Goal: A Process of On-going Improvement*, 3rd ed. (Great Barrington, MA: North River Press, 2012).
7. William Bridges, *Managing Transitions: Making the Most of Change*, 3rd ed. (Philadelphia: Da Capo Press, 2009).
8. Ibid., 4–5.
9. Ibid., 37.

10. Ibid., 25.
11. Ibid., 26.
12. Ibid., 27–28.
13. Ibid., 28–30.
14. Ibid., 30–31.
15. Ibid., 32–33.
16. Ibid., 32.
17. Ibid., 33.
18. Ibid., 34.
19. Ibid., 34–35.
20. Ibid., 36.
21. S. A. Bent, comp., *Familiar Short Sayings of Great Men* (Boston: Ticknor & Co., 1887), Bartleby.com, http://www.bartleby.com/344/137.html.

## Chapter 10, Planning with Motivation in Mind

1. James MacGregor Burns, *Leadership* (New York: Harper Torchbooks, 1978), 420.
2. Kennon L. Callahan, *The Future That Has Come: New Possibilities for Reaching and Growing the Grass Roots* (San Francisco: Jossey-Bass, 2002), 36.
3. Bill Hybels, *Courageous Leadership* (Grand Rapids: Zondervan, 2002), 81–85.
4. John P. Kotter, *Leading Change* (Boston: Harvard Business School Press, 1996), 57.
5. Robert H. Craig and Robert C. Worley, *Dry Bones Live: Helping Congregations Discover New Life* (Louisville, KY: Westminster/John Knox Press, 1992), 68–69.

# Index

Extend your learning and application of this book's contents through web-based resources found at

*www.choosingchange.ca*

This website provides links to

- Additional materials, such as A Theology of Motivation (a web-based chapter from this book)
- Readiness questionnaires that can be downloaded and printed
- Videos and reference materials referred to in this book
- Further explorations of concepts from motivation psychology, including video illustrations of the concepts
- … and I hope a growing collection of stories of congregations that embraced their motivation to change.

You will also find here postings regarding my new learnings about congregational motivation which emerge from my work as a consultant and executive coach to clergy and congregational leaders.